Lessons From a
Red Convertible

Richard W. Dow

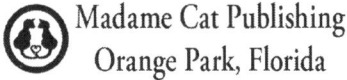
Madame Cat Publishing
Orange Park, Florida

Book design by Frances Keiser of Sagaponack Books & Design

Cover art by Rose Grier Evans

Scripture quotations are from the New Revised Standard Version Bible, copyright 1989, Division of Christian Education of the National Council of the Churches of Christ in the United States of America. Used by permission. All rights reserved.

ISBNs:
978-0-9983859-4-5 (softcover)
978-0-9983859-3-8 (hard cover)
978-0-9983859-5-2 (e-book)

Library of Congress Catalog Card Number: 2018906137

Summary: A collection of essays and sermons written by Pastor Richard Dow, from his perspective as a husband, father, and friend.

REL006110: Religion\Biblical Meditations\General
REL012040: Religion\Christian Life\Inspirational
REL082000: Religion\Christianity\Lutheran

www.MadameCatPublishing.com

First Edition

Printed in the USA

Acknowledgments

A long time ago when I was very young, a pastor I loved and respected delivered a sermon on the woeful state of affairs we'd reached, all current ills coming to a head with the popularity of the new Peggy Lee hit, "Is That All There Is?" I think her song was supposed to offend. I thought I was kind of like a prayer. Who was right? Later on in High School, Mr. Adam taught me how to read a story with perception. Pastor Chet taught me how to tell a story without using too many religious clichés, get to the point, and make it mean something. My wife kept insisting that every story made common sense. My friend John helped me know how to get to the heart of a complex message. I've had good teachers in each of my parishes as well. After all that coaching, I guess all I can tell you is when you hear a story, always ask, "Is that all there is?" and never settle for less than what God is doing there. It works for me.

For my wife and children, who understand
why I love to match unusual stories with
spiritual insights, if that's what they may be.
Their love made it worth the trying.

Contents

Preface

Parking Problems

The best way to explain this "lesson" is to tell you that it started in a cemetery and ended on a sidewalk on a hot summer day. One of the marks of coming of age in 1969 was getting your driver's license. The hardest part of getting ready for the state driver's examination for me was parallel parking. I had a friend who told a story of his driver's test, filled with shame and scolding, when he was asked to parallel park his mom's Buick.

We had an Oldsmobile. Same difference. All summer long I consumed large segments of my mother's free time making her take me to the cemetery across the street from our house, easing the big car over to the curb with terrible lack of accuracy. Finally, my mother gave me an ultimatum. "Either take the driver's test or don't, but the time has come to try." So, I made the appointment, took the test, and got my license. The ultimatum in the cemetery has served me well in the following decades. Conquer your fears; make your move, take the test. You can do it.

Later that summer we took our annual family trip to Williamsburg, Virginia. My sister and I were still young enough to try sliding through the secret gap in the gate that led to the Governor's Mansion and the wondrous maze. The ginger cookies at the old bakery were free then. It was an easy summer to make the transition from childhood to what lay beyond.

One afternoon, my mother and I took a trip downtown. There were colonial-styled buildings for bookshops, tourist gifts and knickknacks, and upscale clothing. My mom led us from the scorching hot sidewalk into the cool confines of a very fancy department store. Mother wanted to buy a scarf for some reason. Since she didn't spend money foolishly, she should have been taken for a serious shopper.

Instead, the distinguished clerk at the scarf counter gave my mother the once over, assessing her incorrectly. The clerk said, "The kind of scarf your kind wants isn't in a store like this. You might want to try a dime store." We got the point easily. We were back out on the sidewalk in an instant, nursing our hurt feelings and sense of shock.

Parallel parking is an art form, as I learned in the cemetery. Now I was learning it in a different way. The quality of your life, the content of your humanity, not to speak of the scuff marks on your mother's Oldsmobile, are about what you learn to align yourself with. Petty snobbery aligns itself with more cosmic forms of hatred, as we were about to see.

As mom and I were standing on the sidewalk in front of the store that was too good for us, a crowd formed around yet another incident. And it was about parallel parking.

Parking spaces in downtown Williamsburg were always at a premium, and still are. So, when one of them became vacant in front of the department store, several drivers slowed and positioned themselves to take it.

Instead, out of nowhere, an enormous 1959 red Cadillac convertible glided effortlessly into a space that I would have guessed would have accommodated a Volkswagen, maybe. There was no backing up, no second-guessing position and trajectory of the car via rear view and side mirrors. The red convertible just swooped right into the available space as if it were the most natural thing in the world. This, though, was not what drew the sidewalk crowd together. The fact that all four of the young men in the car were African American galvanized all passersby into a group on the pavement.

I know what you are thinking. But hold on; there's more. A beautifully dressed lady walked up to my mother, preparing to confide in her. Looking at the car and its occupants, the lady said, "Well, I guess we have to give 'em our parking spaces, but we don't have to love 'em."

Again, I know what you are thinking. In the forty years since my mother and I witnessed the elegance of the red convertible and its parallel parking move, things haven't changed. I fear they may have gotten worse. We don't like people who are different than we are. We don't like it when we think those "different" people may have worked out ways to parallel park their way into our secure worlds. When we spend time trying to decide who belongs in those places of security and who does not, we suppose that we are in control. And, we suppose incorrectly, and to our peril. Why?

Because those who try to decide who to sell a scarf to (and who may not purchase one as well, and why) and those who declare that we do not have to "love" those who boldly move into our worlds are wrong. They are wrong not because they have misjudged the balance of power. They are wrong because they do not know how to parallel park properly. This may not have been precisely what you are thinking. But this notion is worth a second thought.

I began my life as an adult learning the art of parking correctly in a cemetery. There, no one can judge you. You are free to perfect your technique. No one says a word. It's safe there.

I delved deeper into the meaning of parallel parking that hot day in my beautiful, beloved Williamsburg, with my wonderful mom. We both agreed that the surprising, spontaneous elegance of the red convertible taking the parking space was better than making any judgments about who did it or who ought to be there. And we did so in a world where it is not always safe to say that this is what you believe. We found the words, nevertheless. We said, "Nice work, guys." When they laughed in response, so did we. We had aligned ourselves with the daring, the spontaneous, those who showed themselves to be free spirits. It felt good.

Let me make my meaning clear. The world is filled with virtuosos, team players, leaders, followers, dreamers and doers, who all have one wonderful thing in common. They have spent precious time, energy, and hope being the best, the most elegant, the most motivated, and the most joyous ones they can be. And they get better every day. Those people make up the world that I love, and that God loves. Jesus was one. He did it all with discipling walks, deep and delicious wit, and selfless dedication. He could have parked that Cadillac in one move, no sweat. In a way, he was in the red convertible with those four guys, enjoying the ride, I know.

And I know one more thing. Parallel parking means aligning yourself with the best in life. Like parking a big red convertible flawlessly, no matter what people think. One day, when I master the art of parallel parking for myself, I want to be like them.

Pastor Richard W. Dow

1

TIME AND LOVE

Matthew 24:42

Keep awake, therefore, for you do not know the day your Lord is coming.

I know what Jesus is talking about, God. He's talking about when we wait and wait and wait for encouragement, for things to get better, for some indication that you've taken charge again, and we start getting tired. And we stop waiting, and we're going to miss it when you come. Help us hold on a little longer. Amen.

It was getting close to Christmas in northern Illinois in the year 1988. It was the coldest winter in memory, with temperatures that reached the fifty-degree-below-zero mark from time to time. It always felt cold.

A bunch of us decided to get in our cars and drive out into the country. It seemed that a farmer had converted his 1936 farmhouse into a Christmas house. We would be able to look into the windows and see scenes from Santa's home life. There would be a nativity scene, and a children's playhouse, complete with moving, working figures inside. The newspaper said that there were close to a million

Christmas lights decorating the house. Sure enough, we could see the glow miles away.

We got to the house and parked. With our coats buttoned to the chin, gloves and mufflers and hats on, we walked towards the house. It was the essence of holiday charm, and the lights were remarkable. But it was cold. I was cold. After fifteen minutes, I lost feeling in my feet. After twenty minutes, my nose hurt. I remember reading an article in a newspaper somewhere about someone's eyes freezing. I blinked, just to make sure.

I said, "Let's go." The others replied, "No! Look, Santa is so cute. And the reindeer move! Let's stay a little longer!"

There was hot chocolate waiting back at the house. There was also a furnace, and walls and doors to keep in the heat. I thought only of my comfort, not the tenderly beckoning faces of the figures in the nativity scene. I had lost interest in seasonal piety. I wanted to be warm again, if possible.

After thirty-five minutes of excruciating sub-zero Christmas wonder, party time was over. My wife, friends and I were soon in the car with the heater blasting., The car seats were frozen and stiff—and so were we. Nothing could have made me wait a second longer. Nothing.

There's a problem in Matthew's gospel. The problem is that even in warm climates, it is hard to wait for God. It is hard to wait for Christmas, perhaps, but it is becoming extremely difficult to wait for Jesus to return for his second coming. The dream has turned cold, and people just want to go home, living normal lives within the comforts of their home. No more waiting.

So, Matthew remembers. He is remembering the time when Jesus said that the kingdom would come in a moment, with no notice. Beware! Look out! The trouble with such statements is that they keep you on edge. The only thing worse than an edgy Christian is one who has, at heart, lost interest in Jesus and what he will do.

You know the warnings, though.

Two working together in the field, one taken, (the Rapture) while the other remains.

And:

A homeowner can't know when the burglar is coming, so pay attention.

And (the best one):

When Noah was building the ark, people were having fun and enjoying life sanely and normally, until the waters of the flood began to interfere. By then, of course, it was too late.

It will be just like that when Jesus comes back, so, watch out!

As you can probably tell, these words are not my favorites. I don't like being edgy, nervous—is this the end of time? Are these the signs? Maybe this is it! No—I don't like it, and don't normally think that way at all. I am a sensible person, more prone to the normal patterns and rhythms of everyday life than to being alert for the end of time. Time is for using sensibly, for work and play in moderation, not staying on 'red alert' for the second coming. Do you agree?

However, Matthew, in his gospel writing, knows that we are living in a world gone cold for Christ, barely holding on to the expectation that Jesus will come again and apply the finishing touches to his new kingdom. Yes, a church in a world gone cold for Christ has to figure out how to keep watching for Jesus.

One fall, I had to make a kind of a decision along those lines. Let me tell you about it.

I once had a close friend. We worked together in youth ministry—retreats, trips, and the like. We helped guide the congregation's Stephen Ministry program together for a long time. She and her husband were faithful friends when my family was in crisis, and we tried to do the same for her family.

Once I noticed that every time my friend took communion at church, she would say, "Come, Lord Jesus."

When she did it, I thought I had the answer to everything I've ever wondered about why Jesus told us to stay on the alert for him. It's just a matter of knowing Jesus is with you, and then asking him to be with you even more, to a greater degree. So, I started saying "Come, Lord Jesus" when I received communion.

But, that particular fall, I hadn't heard from my friend in a long time. She was busy, so was I. We lived in different states, had different challenges. In fact, I'll bet we hardly knew each other anymore. So, one Sunday as I was receiving communion, I didn't say, "Come, Lord Jesus."

Why not?

I was beginning to think that friendship, love, building the kingdom of God with others, and the best of times might be in the past. Well, living in a world that has grown cold for Christ, you can get a chill yourself. Time goes by, things change, and the love of friendship, even the love of Christ, cools. Live with it. So, I didn't say, "Come, Lord Jesus" anymore.

I was in trouble. Any Christian can do it. I mean, any Christian can find himself or herself in a world that has grown cold for Jesus Christ, and find that your heart has grown cold, too.

That's when Matthew remembers how once Jesus told us to watch, to stay alert, to warm up again to the fact that Jesus will return to us. It could be now, or it could be another thousand years. But he is coming back.

That can keep us warm in a cold world. It can bring mechanical reindeer to life, and it can make us curious again about a nativity scene that has been commercialized to within an inch of its original truth and tender power.

It can keep us believing that life has a good purpose. Where waiting and love intersect, in the act of receiving some bread and wine, we know that Jesus is here. Asking for Jesus to fill our lives just a little more with the ancient words, *Come, Lord Jesus* is a way to keep warm in a world gone cold on Jesus, and to warm others too. Come, Lord Jesus. We are still waiting.

2
ADVENT IN A STATION WAGON

Luke 21:36

> *Be alert at all times, praying that you may have the strength*
> *to escape all these things that will take place, and to stand*
> *before the Son of Man.*

Jesus, you say that we ought to have a kind of spiritual garage sale,
getting as much worry and dissipation out of our lives as possible. So that
we can live in expectation that you will come. I'll make the signs, Lord.
You tell me what to put in the sale. This time, I would really like to clear
out my mind and heart and live to see what you will do. In Your holy
name. Amen.

Do teenagers still drive around on Friday nights? Or is gas too
expensive? My friends and I used to take my dad's station
wagon (with his knowledge and blessing), have a quick dinner,
do some shopping (downtown department stores, built before the turn
of the century!) and then drive. Drive and talk. Drive and dream out
loud. What would the future be like? What would college be like?
What did we expect of marriage? And yes, what was the matter with
the church? Poor old church! Always criticized, or so it seemed.

Then, because the moon was full, or some other reason, I turned the steering wheel. The station wagon, fully occupied with friends, made its way up a steep hill and out into the countryside. At about 190th Street, I turned the wheel again. We were out in the country. There was corn, more corn, and the sky. There was nothing going on out in the ubiquitous cornfields, so we looked up at the sky. There it was, the constellations, the moon that was full, and some planes flying around. And, one really big thing that was maybe a star—no, not a plane—so what was it?

Someone ventured that it might be the second coming.

After all, we're supposed to be waiting for it all the time. In fact, we're supposed to be expecting it, and, like Jesus said, getting ready. The to-do list is probably still ringing in your ears. No drunkenness. No dissipation. And, my personal, unattainable favorite, no worrying!

We sat on the hood of my dad's station wagon and talked about how we felt about the second coming. What would Jesus' perfect world be like? Would we like it? Would it welcome us, or judge us?

And the big question: Were we really ready?

I'd like to tell you that a feeling of peace descended on us as the light in the sky changed shape and, maybe, its distance from us. But, humans being humans, we honestly found that we weren't ready. Come, Lord Jesus, and bring your kingdom with it. But, not quite yet. Not anytime soon, to be honest.

And so, Jesus being the gentleman that he is, did not bring his second coming that night or, so far, any other just yet.

So, in late November, we've got this whole Advent season to deal with where for four long weeks, we sing and pray and preach about the coming of Jesus, once, in Bethlehem and again at the end of time. Come, Lord Jesus. We hope it sounds welcoming, but just what are we singing and praying for?

When I wrote this piece and was serving as an Interim Pastor to a congregation, this was going to be centered around expectations about Jesus coming to the church I was serving in the form of a new pastor. I had high hopes for this writing. We could talk about types of pastoral leadership, and I could even throw in some stories about pastors I have known ... and pastors I have been.

But the whole thing fell apart when I realized something. It is not that we don't want Advent to be fulfilled. That's old news and a part of our fallen humanity that Jesus already knows all about. Yet He is still willing to work with us.

All right, then. What do we spend those four weeks doing, as we light our Advent wreaths and pray the prayers that have the word "stir up" in them? The ancient prayers say things like, "Stir up your power, Lord Jesus, and come. Stir us up. Get us expecting things from you."

It's my belief that the people who put these prayers together long ago knew some important things about Advent, about waiting for Jesus, and what that waiting means. Yes, just as Jesus says, we put aside—what was it—drunkenness, dissipation, and worry. We ask that God get us stirred up about other things. The word I'd like to choose for that is ... discernment. Stir us up, Lord, to be discerning.

If Advent can happen in a station wagon, Advent can happen in a house. My house. At the time, this was a house that was in a group of three houses at the bottom of a ravine. Each house was built into a different part of a hill. At least two of these structures had physical characteristics that reflected their owners' lives. How do I say that? Let's call it discernment. The house next door had a big crack in the rear retaining wall, which was made of cement. That was the wall that kept the hill out of the house. This fissure was so big that a normal person could put their hand inside it, if a normal person goes around putting their hands in cracked walls.

The owners had troubles, too. To make it brief, the wife made too many trips to Chicago to go to parties with famed sports figures. He reacted by drinking too much at parties and showing off a personality that was not too nice. The crack in their lives was, finally, regrettably, a divorce.

How about our house? A similar fault in our cement retaining wall was corrected during the building process with a system of buttressing walls and exterior anchors in the hillside. We were always wondering whether this would work and keep things stable. So, everything became an act of discernment, of reading the signs and deciding what they meant.

So, was it a sign when the workers went on strike while our house was being built? Remember, Jesus said not to worry. So, we moved beyond that. Was it a sign when my mother tried driving us to school one day and slid on the ice right off the crescent-shaped driveway? She thought so at the time. We finally sold the house to a psychiatrist who liked to give lavish barbecues. He wasn't a tidy man about his parties or much else, so his wife left him. A pattern? Who knows? When he finally sold the house, the new owner called my father at work one day.

The owner wanted to know what the floors were made of. Yes, that's right. What the floors were made of. Actually, they were solid oak, but too many barbecues had covered them up and paved them over with grime. The new owners wanted to know if it would be worth the effort to refinish them.

A simple act of discernment (curiosity, conversation, research, and a decision) brought wonderful results.

A different sort of essay might wish to talk about all those barbecues, with some dissipation and drunkenness thrown in. Don't think that hasn't been tempting over the years. But that's not the focus, at Advent, or any other time.

Our focus should be one of prayerful discernment, consisting of curiosity, conversation, research, and decisions. After all, the church is a house as well, a house for God, built of people and hope and yes, even love. So, to get things stirred up, we pray, "Stir up your power, Lord, and come."

When my friends and I sat on the hood of my dad's car in the middle of a cornfield, looking up at something God may have been sending us, we were being asked to discern something. What did it mean for us and for the future? We are still asked to do that, now.

3

SHE SINGS THE IMPOSSIBLE

Luke 1:46–48

> *And Mary said, "My soul magnifies the Lord, and my spirit rejoices in God my Savior, for he has looked with favor on the lowliness of his servant."*

Father, when people find the strength to sing to you, your kingdom comes alive. For instance, Elizabeth. For instance, Mary. For instance, us. "Warm up those voices," you say to us. The kingdom of peace and joy is almost here. Let's sing about it. In Christ's name we pray. Amen.

The Broadway musical *West Side Story* was coming to Jacksonville. Curiously, they were advertising it as perhaps the greatest musical ever. Maybe they were right.

After all, it was a smash hit when it premiered. It has songs like "The Jet Song." ("When you're a Jet, you're a Jet all the way, from your first cigarette, to your last dyin' day.") What else? "One Hand, One Heart"; "I Feel Pretty" (don't count on me to sing that one), and so on. What else? Oh, yes. It was directed by the great Jerome Robbins, and the music was written by the equally great Leonard Bernstein. And, I almost forgot, it was based on Shakespeare's *Romeo and Juliet*.

I like the song called "Somewhere". The girl from one gang falls in love with a guy from a rival gang. Their love, obviously, doesn't stand a chance. The wedding reception alone would put a stop to all their dreams. Their families don't get along. Well, it's more. These two warring families want to kill each other over their turf. Not a good start for a marriage.

So, the girl sings the "Somewhere" song to her guy twice. Once when they fall in love, and once when he's dying in her arms following a gang war.

She sings the impossible.

Here's how it goes:

> *"There's a place for us,*
> *Somewhere a place for us.*
> *Peace and quiet and open air*
> *Wait for us*
> *Somewhere.*
>
> *There's a time for us,*
> *Someday a time for us,*
> *Time together with time to spare,*
> *Time to learn, time to care,*
> *Someday!*
>
> *Somewhere*
> *We'll find a new way of living,*
> *We'll find a way of forgiving*
> *Somewhere …*
>
> *There's a place for us,*
> *A time and place for us.*
> *Hold my hand and we're halfway there.*
> *Hold my hand and I'll take you there*
> *Somehow,*
> *Someday,*
> *Somewhere …"*

A young girl singing a song about the impossible over her dying boyfriend. She won't give up on her dream, even though she sees it dying in her arms. Okay, then, maybe it **is** the greatest musical ever, *West Side Story*.

Luke packs his gospel with music. John the Baptist has a message written in verse. I wonder if he sang it? Maybe. I even hope so. There is Elizabeth's song, which is like the solos that Hannah and Sarah get to sing in the Old Testament. Both are about older women who really want children but have had to face the fact that it's never going to happen. Or is it? Don't be so sure. Be careful what you sing for.

Elizabeth, an old lady, gives birth to a son, John the Baptist. Since Luke is a pretty good musical writer, he shows us what happens when she greets her pregnant cousin, a girl named Mary. She is filled with the Holy Spirit, and sings, sings, sings: "Blessed are you, and blessed is that little baby inside you."

Also, Luke is careful to say that Elizabeth sings in a "big voice."

If you've ever been to a Broadway show, or a road company version, you know that actors playing ordinary people open their mouths and this enormous sound comes forth. But Luke knows his people pretty well. They aren't play-acting anything. This is for real. The Holy Spirit magnifies Elizabeth's voice, so that her little song takes center stage. "Blessed are you, Mary, and blessed is that little baby inside you."

Is there applause? You'd think so, but before it can start, Mary sings her song. It's called the Magnificat, from the opening verse of her song. She sings the previously impossible.

> *"My soul magnifies the Lord. My spirit rejoices in God my savior. For he has looked with favor on the lowliness of his servant."*

The song takes a turn that you might not expect, right in the middle.

> *"God has shown strength with his arm; he has scattered the proud in the imagination of their hearts. He has*

brought down the powerful from their thrones and lifted up the lowly.

"He has filled the hungry with good things and sent the rich away empty. He has helped his servant Israel, in remembrance of his mercy."

There's a little more. Is Mary singing in her big voice, like Elizabeth? My guess is that things get awfully quiet, but that in her small, untrained voice, Mary manages to magnify the Lord, or make God big.

Mary knew something that maybe we don't. When God writes the songs, they are always about something that's really going on, not some dreamy stuff that sounds nice, but people already know they can't depend on. No, Mary's song is about something real.

For instance, Mary might be thinking about history. In Micah, there's another song that sounds like Mary's. In it, the promise from God is that the little countries, like Israel, will be raised up and protected, even though big nations like Assyria want to conquer them. God will protect you and give you what we would call our daily bread.

Does God really protect his people? I'm sorry, but sometimes the greatest musical in the world can't quite convince me. The evidence against it is just too overwhelming. Of course, I'm talking about the violence, injustices, and evil in the world. What about God's promises to lift the lowly, bring down the power-hungry, and protect his people with grace and mercy? I don't feel like singing that song today. Perhaps it's a little late for promises. Or, well … listen to this.

When studying for the ministry, I was assigned nine weeks of work and study in a citywide trauma hospital. Sometimes, that meant staying in the hospital overnight to be on call. During one of those nights, the phone in my room rang. I was up, out, and on my way to the emergency room. There, a family wept. It was inevitable that they were losing their dad to a heart attack. The grown son and daughter-in-law sat with their mom. We talked. There were things that needed to be said about the quality of their family life, some key memories, and some prayers.

The hours seemed to stack on top of one another, weighing us down, and the night. The doctor came and announced that it was all over.

The son cried bitterly, in choking sobs. His wife put her arms around him. Then, the wife of the man who had died spoke. She spoke softly, to no one in particular, or perhaps to God. And to me. In one of those privileged moments when you are allowed to see into the heart of another person, she began to talk, softly.

She said, "You know, I always have a song. Something that I'm singing to myself or humming out loud. Sometimes it's a hymn, but usually it's a pretty song from a show or the radio. I always have a song. But not now. I don't have a song anymore."

We prayed. But there was no song. Silence in the heart.

About a month later I was doing rounds in the hospital, and they said a letter had come for me. It was a greeting card from the widow without a song, thanking me for being with her family. Then, in a small, written postscript at the bottom of the card, she had written, "I have a song again. Thank you."

Elizabeth once believed that God had nothing more for her. But he had a song and a child for her. Mary once thought that God had gotten confused and given her a burden, not a gift.

Instead, her child would come to bring salvation. A song and a child, once again.

There's plenty to convince us that God's song-writing days are over. Elizabeth sings, "Blessed are those who believe."

There's still plenty to convince us that God's song-writing days are over. Mary sings, "He has helped his servant Israel, in remembrance of his mercy."

There's still plenty to convince us that God's song-writing days are over. That the best we can do is cradle a dying dream in our arms and sing, "Somewhere." Strangely, the song that I just can't get out of my head is about God's Savior-son being born in the here and now, for us.

4

ANGRY DUDE IN PRAYER

Luke 9:28–29

> *About eight days after Jesus said this, he took Peter, John, and James with him and went up onto a mountain to pray. As he was praying, the appearance of his face changed, and his clothes became as bright as a flash of lightning.*

Father, what could be easier? Jesus commands us to pray. He gives us words to pray that are always good, always appropriate. We can talk to you all we want. Maybe what's missing here are some listening skills on our part. Lord, teach us how to pray. And that includes listening. In Christ's name, Amen.

I was angry. I was angry with myself. I was angry with the bishop's office. I was angry with God, too. One angry dude.

I had checked the box on my bishop's report form that said that I was available to talk about another call, which meant moving to another church. After all, it had been nine years in one place, and I was wondering if I had done all I really could there.

And what do you know? God took me up on my offer. He gave me the opportunity to move out of Dallas to a medium-sized city in northern Louisiana. Here is something that will tell you about the end of this story. At my Dallas church's farewell party, the cake had the word "Shreveport" in script, with a question mark at the end. Very funny.

I was angry with God. My prayers were angry prayers. I would pray stuff such as "Dear God, thanks for nothing. My dream my whole life long was to live in a big city with a good symphony, in a nice house in a good neighborhood with great schools for the kids. Now, you want me to leave?" By the way, I just threw in the part about the schools to make myself sound more noble.

Who was I kidding? God had my number. One angry dude, praying away. After the lament part of the prayer—which kept getting whinier all the time—I had a question. I asked, "God, what is your will for my life? Should I stay in Dallas, or go to Shreveport?"

I doubt if I was actually talking God senseless. That would take a lot of talking, don't you think? But I was certainly giving it a try. Surely, you've noticed the problem. I was all talk, and no listening.

This was causing problems. I had gone on an outing with my son that weekend, and nearly backed into another car. Another "almost" accident happened as well.

Yet another crisis came in the form of a large manila envelope in the mail one day. It was from the Shreveport church, and it included a large picture of their worship space. "This is beautiful," I said. "Now what am I going to do?" Maybe whine some more. Instead, I went for a run, which is what I did in those days when I had to sort things out. I still remember.

Angry dude lays it on the line in prayer. "Jesus, I can't make up my mind. Dallas or Shreveport? Which should it be? I need a sign." This sort of thing was new for me, since my only approved Lutheran experience up to that point was singing dry, theological hymns, not asking for signs.

Jesus seemed to reply. His reply was compassionate and respected my ability to think and choose. It sounded like this: "*Wherever you go, I will go with you. Stay faithful.*" And that was it. And I was able to make up my mind and take another stab at staying faithful.

Listening, really listening could well be a part of prayer. Here are two ideas about listening from a previously angry dude in prayer.

First, listen to God. In the story of Jesus' transfiguration, I'll admit that there is plenty going on. Jesus goes up the mountain to pray. I actually went up the same mountain once in a taxi, and it took nearly an hour. Walking up this mountainous mountain shows real commitment to prayer. Amid Jesus' clothes glowing from within and brightly, amid the windy clime of the mountaintop, amid the appearance of the talking cloud, Jesus got it right.

God wants to talk to Jesus, as well as hear what *he* has to say. Here God calls his son "my Chosen." It's a different name than God used in Jesus' baptism, and shows that his work of saving us is progressing. Jesus listens. He gets it right and gets to hear what God has to say. It gives him strength and he needs it. The story opens with Jesus talking with Moses and Elijah about his upcoming cross. Jesus needs all the strength he can get, and he gets strength in prayer by being a listener.

The disciples, sadly and to no one's surprise, don't get it. Instead, there is talking, talking, and more talking from Peter, James, and John. Do not blame them. We all do it. And what do they talk about? Building some *thing* to keep the wind out and a fantastic religious experience in. It's not a bad idea. But it comes from their human experience and needs, while God has something distinctly different to say. God keeps it short. He tells disciples, "Listen. Listen to Jesus." Open your ears. Close your mouths. Listen.

Evidence has it that the disciples kept on missing the point for some time. Jesus got more than a little hot under the collar when the disciples tried to heal a demon-possessed child and couldn't do it. Chances are (and this is my guess) they were still thinking about themselves instead of God's presence to heal the little guy. Jesus has little patience with that then and now. There are people to be healed of things. There are Words from God to be enacted with our heads, hearts, and hands. Listening, as Jesus knows, can transfigure a lot of things to show God's glory. And, not just his robes on a mountain somewhere.

There are all sorts of helpful hints about good listening. One is, stop talking. Here's something: Mother Teresa went for over a decade feeling like God wasn't taking her calls anymore, so to speak. That's tough. Keeping your ears open while praying requires faithful toughness sometimes. We don't know the value of this. We just know it is true.

What else? Ask questions for clarification, even with God. Do the speaker the honor of trying to really understand.

One last thing. This has always bothered me, and the Transfiguration hasn't made this any better. Religious listening has transformed the normal person into something pretty nutty sometimes. Do I really want to be clear about what God is saying to me? I'll let you think about that one while I tell one more story.

In the 1930s there was something called the Great Depression. All sorts of terrible things started to become a normal part of people's lives—like not eating. Enter, then, another angry dude in prayer. This time it was a guy in Wisconsin, a Catholic priest. He had gotten ahold of some forest land and was going to clear it for one use or another. But he happened to ask God what his take was on all this land. According to the tourist guide, God asked the priest to build a shrine to God and the Virgin Mary, with gift shop, out of cement and shards from broken glass bottles.

We toured this place back in the 1970s, and I kept thinking, *"No, no, no, no, no, and no. This is dumb. Listening for God in life is not a great idea."*

Then, I calmed down. As I walked, a light snow started to fall, softening the lines of all things made of cement and broken glass. I thought of this priest, fitting each piece together, forming the concrete, and asking himself with some frequency why he was doing it. Suddenly, this sounded more like my life than I was expecting.

Fitting the broken pieces together, as God suggests, and God directs, seeing what can come of it. This is what happens, I thought, when an angry dude in prayer can listen for God.

5

EMPTY AWAY

Luke 1:53

God has filled the hungry with good things and has sent the
rich away empty.

Heavenly Father, we are waiting for the birth of Jesus. We are hungry
for his saving grace. Fill us with good things. Amen.

That's what Mary is singing about. That's the kind of singing
you do when you know Jesus is coming, and that you're
going to be a witness to getting him here. That's the kind of
singing you do. "God has filled the hungry with good things and has
sent the rich away empty."

By the way, you won't find those religious song lyrics on my
Christmas cards this year or any other year. He has sent the rich
away empty and filled the hungry with good things.

That's not my Christmas song. But Mary keeps singing it, and it
just won't go away. The hungry get good things, and the rich go away
empty. Mary's song is ringing in my ears.

A long time ago, when we first knew that there were people without
homes, I was taking a youth group to one of the National Youth

Gatherings in a northern city, in the middle of summer. We had a break one day and found ourselves downtown. There was a street with shops and restaurants, and people out having fun. Out of the corner of my eye, I saw a woman dressed in a long wool coat. Her hair was long and wild. She had a sneaky look about her. She just stepped into an alleyway and opened a dumpster. She took some food.

Before she could get away, I asked the kids to look and to tell me what they were seeing.

They had no idea, so I told them that they were looking at a homeless person, who was hungry enough to eat what others had thrown away. "Gross!" they said. And that was all. I had changed nothing for that woman or the Christian kids in my care. We were just tourists looking at a problem from a safe distance. And so, we moved on. *He has filled the hungry with good things, and the rich he sends away empty.* "Is that so?" I thought. "Is that so? Don't count on me to help, or to know how."

In 1990, I flew from my parish in Dallas to Berkeley, California, for two weeks of Stephen Ministry leadership training. Berkeley is a college town, alright, and it is packed to overflowing with college students and with characters. In those days, before they cleaned out the streets and parks, Berkeley was also home to hundreds of homeless people. I would get up with the dawn each day and go for a run. The first day I was afraid because the homeless people were sleeping on the sidewalks. What if one of them got up while I was running past? What then?

After the third or fourth day, I had learned to ignore them, as they had long ago learned to ignore the likes of me. On the day before we graduated as Stephen leaders, I was standing on the balcony of our classroom building, looking down at the homeless, the students, the incredible mix of people that Berkeley is.

The person next to me said, "We've just spent two weeks of our lives and a lot of money learning how to help people, and we will. But what about them? They had to be normal people once. What happened? Wasn't there anyone there to help them?"

And then we graduated, and we went away, and the hungry were still on the streets of Berkeley. If I heard Mary singing her song about being Jesus' mom, I still didn't know how to sing along. Not at all.

Later, I had to write and give a sermon on Mary's song in Luke, Chapter 1. Turns out I had no idea what it was about at all. I wanted to learn. It turns out that in Mary's day, people who believed in God also believed that the rich were rich because they were good enough to get God's favor. They also believed that the poor had it coming to them, because they were not good enough. How do ideas like that get into a religion that also produces the Christ? I don't know. More to the point, how could I learn how to sing Mary's song that turns thinking like that upside down?

Here is how I learned how to sing Mary's song about filling the hungry with good things and sending the rich (could that be me?) away empty.

One Friday morning I brought from home a sack of throwaway stuff that I thought could go in the church dumpster. I threw it in, and to my horror, I saw it land on a homeless person inside. He didn't even wake up. I checked around. He was well known by folks in the neighborhood.

The following Wednesday I was looking for a sermon illustration for our Wednesday worship service and I thought about the man in the dumpster. I talked about him. Everyone agreed that this was a disgraceful thing. We also agreed that a person who was comfortable sleeping in a dumpster was beyond our ability to help. But could we help someone? Were there people for whom we could do something?

It turns out that the chair of the Outreach Committee knew of another church that had found the answer to that question. There was a group of people who had found a way to help families who had lost their homes, but wanted to keep their dignity, stay together, keep their kids in school and get jobs again.

It seemed to me that maybe if people like that were allowed to fall too far, they would end up in a dumpster, and my faith told me that shouldn't happen. My faith told me that if we could help by offering whatever simple, basic riches we had, like food and a clean, safe place to sleep, such as in our church building, and some casual encouragement, as many other community churches had done through this outreach program, then maybe I had discovered the meaning of Mary's long-ago song that I was still hearing.

Maybe what Mary was singing about was that God fills the hungry with good things I have to share, and that when the rich are sent away empty, it's not punishment. It just means that we've given of what we have, and gladly expect to receive a replenished supply from God again. That way, Mary's old, old song is good news for everybody because of the way it turns a world filled with people who don't know how to help those who are down on their luck, well, it turns that world upside down.

Mary's song came alive at that church and we learned how to get involved to help homeless families by working with a community organization and learned to keep singing Mary's song of hope in our hearts. The hungry had been filled with good things, by people like us who went away empty, having given what was needed, and knowing God would give us more. Keep singing in your hearts and listen well to Mary's words of hope.

6
I Knew He Would Come

Luke 2:14

Glory to God in the highest heaven, and on earth peace among those whom he favors.

God of love, we see your son in his sinless beauty as a baby. We see your son later on his cross, conquering our sin. Help us to live the beauty of Christ's birth. Help us live the profound love of what he came to do. In Christ's holy name we pray. Amen.

"I knew someone would come."

That's what the young mother said, standing helpless in the parking lot, the brick walls of the shopping mall rising up behind her. The Dallas summer heat was coming up strong from the pavement beneath her feet, and she was crying.

She had locked her baby in her car. As I came nearer, I could see it was an older kind of Oldsmobile, where you could sometimes pop the lock with a coat hanger wire. "Help me," the mom said, crying in the hot summer sun. "Help me, my baby's in there, in the car."

This was bad. We started to talk fast, back and forth, about where to get a coat hanger and try the lock. This was when the mom remembered the key. She said her grandfather always told her to put an extra car key under the license plate screw. We used a dime as a screwdriver to find out. The baby's cry sounded desperate now. Then the key fell from its hiding place. In an instant the door was open, mother and child reunited.

"I knew someone would come," she said, drying her tears. "I prayed. I knew God would send someone."

The people of God were waiting, in a time before parking lots and malls and cars. The people of God had been waiting since the time of King David. Someone would come.

God would send someone to show them the way, to rescue their children, to dry their tears, to unlock the power of death and sin. Someone had to come.

A few years ago, I was sitting in a hospital room downtown, marking time in the middle of the night. It was the night before my mother died. I would calm her forehead with a cool washcloth and give her a tiny kiss. Her breathing was labored, and it was very hard to tell if she knew I was there. I would look out over the river, at the bridge with the blue lights, imagining that this was the dimension between life and death, a world coated in blue, covered in sorrow. I listened to my mother's breathing. I waited, alone.

"Someone," I thought, "may come. Someone may come to let me know I'm not alone."

At about nine o'clock, someone came. It was a member of our congregation. He talked with me, listening carefully to anything and everything I had to say. He listened to my concerns, and he prayed with me. In the back of my mind I was thinking that he had left the comfort of his home. He had gone out of his way to let me know in person that God cared, and God was there.

After about an hour, I told him to go home and get some sleep. But what he'd done lasted the rest of the night. You see, I knew someone would come. "I knew God would send someone."

It's Christmas Eve—the first one, when nobody knows it's Christmas Eve yet. The baby's just been born. The someone that people still believed God would send? He was here! He came to be loved, and to love, with a love that would break the bonds of death and the power of sin. But since this is the first Christmas Eve, nobody knows that yet. They still live in that cold blue haze of the lonely midnight hour I was talking about before. They don't know.

The shepherds don't know that someone has come, yet. They tend their flocks by day, and by night. They watch for wolves and dangerous cliffs and wandering sheep. This is hard work, lonely and tough, with an unstopping wind across the winter landscape that can dry you out and use you up. Shepherds devoted their lives to caring for the sheep. Maybe that indicated a caring heart, beneath a surface coarseness. Or maybe they were just stuck with those crazy sheep, and what else would they be doing, what choice did they have?

But how long can that last, before someone comes to help, to care for us, and to show the way? How long, before someone comes?

Maybe you are reading this wondering the same thing. You've tried your best with what you have been given. Or maybe you find yourself in some situation that places demands on your faith. It's not what you chose, but you are stuck with it. And, like those shepherds stuck with those crazy sheep, you don't know how much longer you can last. But perhaps someone will come. Someone who brings a fresh approach, or living water, or the genuine touch of God. Come quickly, then, whoever you are. We need you now.

Angels were up late that night, too. They were watching the heavenly news and had a breaking story on their hands. Someone was on the way, at last! They looked at each other and said, "Here we go! King of Kings, Wonderful Counselor, Prince of Peace!"

Then the angels stopped. They knew the people had had enough of the high and mighty. They understood that the people—from princes to paupers—needed a heavenly, holy someone who could be a real part of human life from his first day … to his last. Then they got the rest of the news.

This heavenly, holy, Son of God and Son of Man *someone*, would be a baby, born to very humble parents, in surroundings that would shock even Joseph and Mary—a common stable. The baby would be wrapped in swaddling clothes and lying in a manger. It seemed to the angels that because this holy, human baby had a home and warmth and love in a lowly manger, he might also stand a chance to find the same in people's hearts.

The angels thought they'd better get busy, and so one of them went to the shepherds. An angel realizes he only has so much time to talk, up in the sky with the glory of the Lord all around, and humble shepherds below. So, the angel came to the point. Don't be afraid, go and see. See what? See for yourself that at last, someone has come. God has come. Emmanuel. To you this day is born in the city of David, a savior, who is the Messiah. Look for a baby, in a blanket, in a manger. Got it? Get going. You won't want to miss this. After all that waiting, GO!

Now, the angels are not done yet. People like shepherds and all the rest of us who know what waiting is like, what do we know? There's a lot in the waiting manual about what to do before God comes to us. There are things like have patience, be faithful, and the ever-popular chapter on hanging in there. But there's almost nothing about what to do when you've been hoping someone will come, and that someone finally comes.

The angels tell us what to do. They've written a song, and it goes like this: "*Glory to God in the highest heaven, and on earth peace among those whom he favors.*"

Listen to what the angels sing for a second. They say that the joy and everything else that God the Father and God the Son have together in heaven is now right here. Among us. Among those whom God favors. Does that sound like a last-minute religious trick? Oh, God's *someone* came, but only to people who are nice enough for God? No, that's not it at all.

Pay attention to the angels. The favored ones are the ones who can learn to sing the angels' song. The favored ones are those who can say—or, better, sing—"Thanks, God!"

After all this waiting, you came. Precise location *then*: Bethlehem, stable, straw, with Mary and Joseph. Precise location *now*: my life, my heart. *You came.* And now, no matter what the night may have for me, I'm better than all right. I'm yours. I wait no more. Christ is born. Sin is broken. Death is done. I rest in you, no matter what. I was so tired of waiting, but now I'm yours, and you, in the manger, are mine.

All through the night, keeping watch as my mother slowly let go of life and went to her Lord, I remembered what she would say to me, nearly every day of the last few years of her life. She said that she loved me more than I would ever know. *More than I would ever know.* I always believed what she said, even when I didn't understand fully. But now, in the waiting through the cold blue middle of the night, I understood the same truth about God. He loves me more than I will ever know.

I know because I, like the rest of the world, was waiting for someone to come. And in the middle of the night, with joy and surprise and love, he came. Christ is born.

7
PILATE'S DREAM

John 18:38

"What is truth?" Pilate asked.

Dear Jesus, you are the king of everything. What you say goes. There are only a few places where you are not yet king. There is some territory, rocky and off limits, in our hearts, where you have not yet become king. Someday, you will rule there, not by forcing your way in, but by persisting in loving us until you win. We will know this has happened when we love as you do. That is the truth which you bring. Conquer us with love, Jesus. Bring your truth. Amen.

Last night I had a dream. In my dream, the church I was serving at the time was surrounded by trouble, as if it were on a sea and waves were threatening to toss the crew overboard and then sink the ship. That was the beginning of my dream. But, as this dream continued, the crew began to pitch in. They looked upon each other with compassion. Those who could swim took the work on the outer decks, so that those who could not and were afraid could continue to do what they could in a safer place.

The sea never calmed at all. Instead, it brought others close to the ship we were piloting. For a little while, we thought about ignoring their cries and their needs. But, after all, we were in danger of sinking. Survival was the only order of business. Since those who were strong swimmers were on the outer decks and were not as afraid, they organized ways to help the drowning ones get on board.

The sea never calmed at all. At one point, all of us understood that the sea would never calm. The tossing and turning that we were experiencing was not because there was something wrong with the boat, or with us. It was just the way it is on the sea. We developed what they call sea legs, and we were no longer frightened of the gale or the water. We talked of survival still, but it was now the survival of those around us in the sea who looked like they were drowning. We discovered at last that we had what it took to help them, and to tell them in the name of our Lord not to be afraid. Then I woke up.

When I awoke, there was talk about recession, as if it were a raging sea, waiting to claim us and others. When I awoke, there was anger and fear and even—I couldn't believe it—indifference about the sea around us, about the church itself, and about the Lord who was trying to pilot the ship, which is the church. When I woke up, I discovered that my dream was only that, as the people around me seemed to know only one thing to say: every man for himself!

What is the truth? My dream was of cooperation, of developing sea legs and confidence to care for each other and those in the waters around us. Is truth to be found in waking moments, when cold reality demands that each of us plan and act only for ourselves? I'm not sure.

Pontius Pilate was a dreamer too, although you might not believe it. In his dream, he dreamt that he could have authority without responsibility. You don't believe me? Watch as Pilate speaks to Jesus in his trial for being a messiah in a Roman world, where only Caesar may lead and claim people's allegiance.

Watch Pilate for yourself. During the trial, Pilate asks Jesus once, twice, almost three times whether he is actually a king, a king of the Jews. At another point in the trial, Pilate goes out to the people, the crowd below who move as if they were waves on an angry sea. Once, twice, three times Pilate asks the people below to do his job, to choose between Jesus, the gentle messiah who taught people growth in grace and joy in service, and Barabbas, amateur terrorist who promised the crowd that life is found in putting your own needs first.

As Jesus almost silently turns the tide during the trial, subtly but surely putting his accuser, Pilate, on trial, tell me I'm wrong about Pilate's dream. His dream was that he wanted a life of authority without responsibility. When that dream becomes a reality, someone or something ends up on a cross. Sometimes it's Jesus. Sometimes it's the future of the church. Is Christ a king? Or is Pilate's dream of authority without responsibility the reality? He wonders himself. That's why his hallmark in history is his world-weary question for a patient messiah who may be a king: What is truth?

I should be used to choppy seas surrounding the church by now. And I should be used to the truth that Jesus is the captain of our ship, our king, and that he knows just what he's doing. I should be used to that truth, and that is "truth." Where would you point to locate the truth? The Bible? Good. The Creeds? Good, again. The passionately, immaculately preached sermon? I would agree.

How about a simple act of service, rendered on a violently pitching deck of the ship of the church, surrounded by storm? Is that truth? Or are we allowed on this ship as passengers who speak with authority about what to do during the storm, but without responsibility to help? What is truth?

My first year in the ordained ministry, the economy collapsed. That's why I said I should be used to this by now. Am I? I wonder. I wonder if you ever get used to it. Anyway, the economy collapsed right after I was called as an associate pastor of a medium-sized church.

Next, the nearby Chrysler factory almost closed. People without jobs boarded up homes that wouldn't sell and headed out of town, not looking back. Several big factories closed in the next town. In no time, people were hungry, and without food. There was a big meeting one afternoon, called by the officers of the local Salvation Army, who were the people on the outer decks at that time, the ones closest to the waves, so to speak, hearing the cries of those going under.

The Salvation Army people invited to their meeting people from the local Green Giant packing plant. They invited pastors and the Roman Catholic priest, who turned out to have astonishing organizational skills. They invited members from the local churches, as well. The room was full by the time the first meeting began. Some of us were frightened by the enormity of the task, but we wanted to help.

Of all the varied dreams of the people in that room, not one of us was dreaming Pilate's dream—remember, authority without responsibility. Some of us were dreaming of where our Lord, king that he is and pilot of a rolling, pitching ship, would take us next.

It took us about three months to organize and stock one of the first food pantries we had ever heard of. It was in an old Salvation Army building downtown, a garage, really.

The meetings continued, and I, the inexperienced one, took the minutes, typed them up, and in the proofreading, looked for the truth of the situation we were trying to help. What is truth? And, can truth calm the heart, feed the body, and heal the community? Is Jesus truth, with his gentle leading and serving of all? If his steady obedience to the Father is truth, then how do we get the same for ourselves? What is truth? In which dream do we find it?

A woman from my congregation was one of the full-time staffers of the food pantry. Unemployment rose to twenty percent. There was talk of selling or closing the Chrysler plant. Everyone was on edge. It didn't seem to affect this woman, who had raised seven children and had seen worse times yet, I supposed.

Winter came, with numbing cold that shot through everything and everyone and stayed there. People remembered the time there was so much snow it caved in the roof of the Green Giant factory, because there was almost that much snow again. Things were especially bitter for those without work, without food. The food pantry was busier than ever.

It was so busy that the lady from our church who was always there almost missed the woman who came in, collected the food she was eligible for, and silently, quickly left. Someone said she had no shoes, certainly, they remembered, she had no coat. The lady from our church chased after her and stopped her, bare feet in the snow.

She said, "Child, what are you doing in this freezing cold with no shoes?"

Answer: "I don't have none."

The lady from our church replied without hesitation: "Here, take mine," and the lady from our church walked back to the food pantry shoeless, in the cold snow.

My dream, the one I dreamed last night, was a lot like that. In obedience to our Lord, who lived in loving obedience to his Father, the lady from the church walked back in the snow. The seas around the ship that is the church calmed for a moment, and there was the crisp, clean feeling of truth in the air. That was my dream for the church and continues to be.

8
THE COLOR OF CHRISTMAS

Luke 2:29

Master, now you are dismissing your servant in peace, according to your Word.

Heavenly Father, Jesus is brought to the temple as a baby, prophecies begin, and Mary's soul is cut with a sword. What kind of a messiah did you send us? What kind of son is it that you have? For starters, he's one who shakes things up. Dare we pray, send him to shake things up in our world? In Christ's name we pray. Amen

The door was locked almost all the time. On Monday nights, people went in and out.

The rest of us at church could hear conversation, the silence of people hard at work, and occasionally laughter. What was going on behind that door, in the basement of the church, a door that was locked almost all the time?

They were putting together the image of Christ.

For a long time, the worship space in the church focused on the altar, which was in the middle of a round area. I used to say that preaching and communion were like being on a lazy susan, revolving around in a circle, feeding the congregation. A person can get a little dizzy doing that over a period of time. So, some people in our church decided that the focal point of worship ought to begin at the base of the altar, and visually lead the worshipper up toward heaven. A large, rectangular stained-glass window, about five feet across and about twenty feet high, was planned. It would be backlighted for maximum effect, and it would bear the image of Jesus, the Christ.

The people, members of my congregation and stained-glass artists behind that door were busy, for month upon month, selecting the colors for Jesus' face, for his robe, his hands, and the background behind him. The plans had been made, and now they were being given color, shading, and reality.

That is what is happening in the part of Luke's gospel where Joseph and Mary take the infant Jesus to the temple in Jerusalem. There is a ceremony of dedication for young males of infant age, and that is why they have brought Jesus. There is the sacrifice of certain animals (our modern minds don't picture that very well, but, yes, two animals were sacrificed for Jesus). That is the last time this will occur for Jesus, because the system of temple sacrifice for worship of God was coming to a swift end. From now on, Jesus himself would be the sacrifice. His blood. His life. But not quite yet.

The picture of who Jesus is (and who he will shortly become) is still being completed, like fitting the stained glass into the framework of a window. This time, thanks to Luke, the door is not locked. We can enter easily and see what God is giving us.

The first part of the image of Jesus belongs to Simeon. See him as he puts it into place.

He is old. But he has been living on a promise. The promise is that he will live to see the Messiah in the flesh. Saying it simply, his image of Jesus is that no matter how long you might think you have been waiting, and no matter what you have already waited through in your life, Jesus will come to you. Your waiting will not be in vain. Don't give up. Jesus will come to you.

The second part of the image belongs to Anna, the prophetess. Her message is simple. The words aren't recorded. Just the fact that she speaks is important. In Jesus' new world, everyone has something to contribute, has something of value. Your life is not in vain. You have, by the grace of God, something important to offer.

The third part of the image belongs to Mary. Hers is the most visually jarring. She hears that the world around her will conflict in all kinds of ways with the kingdom her little son is bringing. If I can borrow a cliché from the movies, it's almost like a Western where the good guy tells the bad guy that there isn't enough room in this town for both of us. And it's true. The kingdom of this world and the kingdom of God are not going to sit side by side on this planet, or in your heart. And the kingdom of this world isn't going to go without a fight. As Mary watches that ongoing conflict between the values of this world and the one her son brings, a sword will slash at her heart. Her son's life will cause her pain. Read the passage from Luke again.

In the church basement, the door was finally unlocked. The window, with each part assembled to make an image of Christ, was ready. In a weekend, it was installed in the worship space. The colors chosen were white, yellow, and red. People complained that the picture of Christ was too vivid, even shocking. I knew that the white was carefully selected for purity. The red was chosen for the reality of Christ as a human being and his Godly sacrifice. And the yellow? I'll have to admit that it was the most unpleasant, mustard yellow I had seen in a long time. I wanted to change it to a milder shade.

So, I guess that the yellow in the image of Christ was me. As long as the kingdom of this world is at work in me, changes will need to be made. And when I want to make those changes, Christ is at work. There is hope. Simeon's words, Anna's talk and Mary's pain make sense.

Oh, they do? What image, what stained glass window, what sermon could make you see that waiting and pain make sense?

Maybe, the story of Jesus in the temple.

Maybe, this:

In Louisiana, during Hurricane Katrina, the people began to head north and slowly at first filter into Shreveport, where I was. I received a phone call from a Lutheran pastor in Atlanta who wanted to talk about his sister and brother-in-law. They had been on vacation in New Orleans before the hurricane began.

They got out and were heading for Shreveport. He asked if I could help them get settled. Sure. I would do whatever I could. Then the pastor from Atlanta added, "My brother-in-law is not a Christian. In fact, he fights against the faith. Maybe this time something will happen to show him that God is a part of his life. I don't know. Good luck. Bye."

Now what? A crazy trip out of New Orleans, a deadly hurricane, and me. This was supposed to show him Christ? Good luck.

The couple came and brought along a friend. The couple had watched the water rushing down the street to their hotel lobby like a moving wall. The people inside the hotel lobby started acting ugly. The couple knew it was time to go. They offered people money to rent their cars. No. To buy their cars. No. Finally, they found this guy, who had never been out of the city in his life. His apartment was flooded. He watched in disbelief as a dead body floated by, and knew he was in trouble. The couple and the guy formed a relationship immediately. A relationship of survival.

They would get in his car and get out of the city. Together.

When they got to Shreveport, I said, "I'll go into the evacuee shelter with you, to see if it's okay. If it's not, you can stay at my house."

The couple misunderstood. They thought I meant the offer of our home was just for them, but not the guy who had become their new friend. They told me thanks, but under no circumstances would they be separated from him until they saw him safe and sound at his sister's house in Monroe. They would stay together in the shelter. They would protect him. They were a family now.

I thought about how I was supposed to give them a glimpse of Christ or something, and realized it was too late. They had given me one. I had seen Jesus and his new kingdom in *them*. The whole picture. The old kingdom of selfishness, fear, and sin had been swept away. Just like Simeon said, and Mary knew.

Strange, how that sometimes begins with a wall of water rushing toward you, changing everything, sweeping the old away and bringing the new together to create the whole picture with us the individual pieces, making a picture of Christ.

Today, through that wall of rushing water new life begins, calling us to become part of the picture of Jesus the Christ in this world. The old is gone, the new is come.

9
LOOK AT THE MANGER

Luke 2:10–12

> *But the angel said to them, "Do not be afraid; for see—I am bringing you good news of great joy for all the people: [11]to you is born this day in the city of David a Savior, who is the Messiah, the Lord. This will be a sign for you: you will find a child wrapped in bands of cloth and lying in a manger.*

The stable where Jesus was born was not a pretty sight, God, yet there was beauty. You created that beauty from the obedience of Mary, the servant-hood of Joseph, the silvery song of the angels above, and the wonderment of the shepherds. Help us at all times to see the beauty you created in a manger, where animals feed. Help us at all times to believe that you create the same, a home for yourself, in our hearts. In Christ's name we pray. Amen.

Give me a miracle, not a manger.

That's what I say, and I don't think it could be any clearer, do you?

The extreme humility of the birth of Jesus the Christ makes for excellent telling, but few of us would wish to leave the comforts of now and go home to a stable, troubling livestock around us, to find a place in a crude home in a world that did not want us. Not really.

Give me a miracle, not a manger.

The obedience of the Virgin Mary is matched by the rare and unusual sense of servant-hood in husband Joseph. They know that they are in the presence of the Christ; the Messiah, predicted and longed for. He is born. The example of mother and father inspires me to believe that in the presence of a living Lord, we might rise above what some say we are and others say we have become. Selfishness and the cold shoulder melt away in the presence of the infant king of all creation. Yes, I believe. But still …

Give me a miracle, not a manger.

The shepherds come, inviting each other to come and see the bold and daring thing that God has done. His plan was to save a lost and fallen humanity by becoming one of us, true God and true man in one person, one time, once for all. I close my eyes and imagine myself as one of them, rejected by good Jews and proper people, yet in the beginning moments of the salvation of humankind. At last, those who have given up on being a part of the human race are now at the center of what is best about life, the presence of Christ. I have felt excluded, and I have yearned for this.

I close my eyes and imagine while the story is being read. I am one of them. God is mine, and his love comes down to me, enveloping me, gladdening my heart. This is what I have needed all along.

But still I will say …

Give me a miracle, not a manger.

Christmas should be about my well-being, and the glossy security I want for those I love.

The holiday passes before me in a seamless display of good health, good times, good food, and celebration. Nothing intrudes. My secret prayer for Christmas is this: give me a miracle, not a manger, because there things are uncertain and cold, where the lowly do what they can with so little. Miracles, please. Not a manger.

And it is to me that the gospel of Luke speaks, loud and clear, the message of the manger!

Is it really that bad?

Maybe.

In 1984 my wife and I decided it was time for a change of scene, a vacation. We would take our ten-week-old infant son and drive from northern Illinois to Mackinac Island in northern Michigan. It took a long time to get there. Mackinac Island is a kind of paradise, I guess.

There is the Grand Hotel, which has been in the movies. There are no cars on the island, only horses and the occasional bicycle. You get there by ferry, across water that is chilly in summer, frozen and inaccessible in winter. We made the trip. Our reservations were for a hotel that was less grand than the Grand Hotel, but still nice. We checked in. While I was standing in line with my son in my arms, I overheard the desk clerk explain to an angry family that the pool was broken. People were asking for their money back. No deal.

While I was listening, I was also looking around, specifically up at the ceiling. I saw a bat. Babe in arms. Bat hovering above. Not what I had bargained for. My internal temperature was rising. Did these people think they were running a hotel? Or what?

Our room was at the end of a very, very long corridor. We portaged suitcases, diaper bag, toys, and all the other stuff people take when they go away with an infant, down this long-distance corridor to our room. Oh, no. We forgot. We needed a crib one with the side bars spaced appropriately, like they pictured in *Parents Magazine*. We called the desk: "Sorry. We're out of cribs."

The baby spent the first night of his first vacation sleeping in a dresser drawer. And a lesson is learned. One that will be learned many times again, as another baby comes a few years later. On a snowy night, as we run out of diapers and formula and I write a check for them on a checking account that only has about 68 cents in it. The bank was understanding. Maybe they knew something that we needed to learn. In real life, as at Christmas, the miracle *is* the manger.

The message is that God is with us—that's what Emmanuel means. And God is with us in the mangiest situations. Jesus is living in a small-time shack in Bethlehem, born there on that night long ago. He's with us, bringing peace on earth where nothing was right before he came. All he has to do is show up to make it right, pleased to be with us. That's the miracle. The manger.

I love the Christmas story. What happened to the sheep when the shepherds went to see the baby Jesus? Luke doesn't tell us. Maybe he did not know. He did know that when Jesus came, the usual way of living changed.

I love the Christmas story. What about the way it starts, with the census, the counting of heads in the Jewish province of the Roman Empire that is somehow associated with some governor named Quirinius? What does that mean?

Luke wants to tell us that before we look at the manger, we need to look way off in the other direction to Christmas where it happens in Rome. In Rome, Augustus Caesar sits on the throne as the first emperor. Mark Antony, the only real threat to Augustus, has killed himself after the battle of Actium in 31 BC. Augustus disbands the Roman senate and has his dad, Julius Caesar, declared a god. The idea is to get people to worship Augustus, which they do, if they know what is good for them.

In effect, they're worshipping power. Raw, naked power as incarnated in the Roman Empire and what it can do. It can pave a road, build an aqueduct, or subdue a nation with a skilled and well-organized army. Power is to be worshipped. And the world's religion is something like... give me a miracle, not a manger.

Luke looks at this situation and says the gospel equivalent of "not so fast." There are other things that count, and other things that are there for us to worship. A God who promises that forgiveness is a stronger builder of empires than the sword. A God who sends his heavenly armies to join some scruffy but excited shepherds in a birthday party for a new and different kind of king: One who rules with his healing hand on broken hearts, not with his foot on your throat.

I love the Christmas story. It takes me back to a time when there were bats in the lobby, no crib in the hotel, and no pool at the inn. But love carried the day. It always does, if you worship the right king.

Luke wants us to do that. That's why, unaccountably by any other standards or plan, he mentions the manger three times in twenty verses of his chapter in his book on the king of kings and on what a funny, glorious, flea-bitten night that king came to us. It's serious, and I shouldn't talk about it that way, but I can't help it. Luke knows something important, and he wants to use that simple manger, a feeding trough for some animals, to point to the truth. On Christmas Eve the score is Augustus Caesar, zero; Jesus one, or two or three if you count Mary and Joseph, or maybe ten if you count the shepherds, and more if you count us.

But can Jesus count on us? Where will we end up on Christmas Eve? Wanting another big, glorious miracle of a Christmas, with everything magazine-glorious to show us that we've got the power, that nothing can touch us? Or, how about this? We could end up at the manger, with those no-account shepherds, the hastily put together home that Joseph and Mary made for their little baby, glued together with nothing but the belief that God loves us, and wants nothing more than to be with us, tonight and always, never leaving, no matter what happens. Which Christmas would you like?

Forget everything else. I'll take the manger. Because it is there that Jesus takes my heart.

10
JESUS GETS CONFIRMED

Luke 2:49

> *He said to them, "Why were you searching for me? Did you not know that I must be in my Father's house?"*

Jesus, it looks like confirmation to me. Studying in the temple in Jerusalem as hard as you can. Growing in faith. Growing up in the faith. Taking charge of your faith. The church matures you during that time, and you mature the church now. Keep doing this, Lord, while we pay close attention. In your holy name we pray. Amen.

I told my friends about the Roman Catholic garage sale. It was on a Friday night, and we were in college. We chose to go to the Roman Catholic garage sale instead of all the other things that we usually did.

When we got to my college, St. Ambrose, a venerable Catholic school, the sale was on. We entered the auditorium, where perhaps fifty folding tables were set up. Displayed on them were all sorts of things that a church could accumulate over a century. Well, to tell the truth, there were perhaps a hundred pictures of the Virgin Mary.

In some, she was alone. In all she radiated a mix of wisdom and sadness. What else could she do?

In others, she cradled her infant son. They looked good together. At peace. Most of these pictures were faded and tinged with brown, as if they were very old, and now had to go, to make way for the new. People were buying them. Maybe for the pictures. Maybe for the frames.

There was one "prie dieu" left (most of these prayer kneelers had gone fast, at the beginning of the sale). Before the rest of us could do anything, my friend Dennis bought it. The rest of us wanted it. It looked antique and classy. We began to prowl the aisles for some treasure we could take with us.

The garage sale had turned into a treasure hunt. The woman looking through piles of books was way ahead of us on that one. There she was, looking an indeterminate age, her hair carefully dyed and permed, and World War II Victory Red lipstick on. She was pulling the piles of books apart with her hands. "What are you looking for?" we asked.

"Honey," she replied. "if I have to dig to the bottom of this pile, I'm going to find *Gone with the Wind* if it's the last thing I do."

I do not think she found *Gone with the Wind* at the Roman Catholic garage sale.

The thing is, at a church garage sale (we are speaking figuratively here, from the view of ideas and beliefs) … at a church garage sale, we don't look for what we think we want. That's what the Gone-with-the-Wind-Lady was doing. Digging through piles of religious books to get what she thought she would like. Instead, when we come to church (I left the words garage sale out for clarity) we receive what God has to give us.

But no, that's not really the way it goes, is it? In the church we know, we tell God or the pastor or the church council president what we want. And, by God, we expect to get it. The pictures. The "prie dieu". The copy of *Gone with the Wind*. Whatever we want, the church garage sale better have it.

I'm like this. Long after we talked with the Red Lipstick Lady, I was still pawing through all the stuff, looking for what I wanted: what I thought would make me happy.

I must have been out of my mind. The church doesn't really work that way, and I don't think God does, either.

Instead of you and me pawing through a stack of religious ideas and images, seeing which ones work for us and which don't, there's something else. The pros call it "revealed faith." What that means is that we can't really know anything true about God unless he talks to us about it. Garage sales are interesting, I guess. So is the idea of coming to church and getting exactly what you want. But if you want a mature faith, one with some backbone to it, you have to listen to what God has to say. Wait for what God has to offer, his gifts of life.

If the Roman Catholic garage sale had a real sale, the kind with people receiving free gifts from God instead of paying for stale artifacts, then there would have been a table with seven sacraments. Free gifts from God for the people of God, with grace and love more profound and lasting than any shopper could find on their own.

Seven sacraments in the Roman Catholic garage sale for free, from God to us. Baptism, Confirmation, Holy Communion, Confession, Marriage, Holy Orders, and the Anointing of the Sick. That's most appropriate for a Roman Catholic event, but what about Lutherans? Martin Luther had a huge problem when it came to the sacraments. By the way, a sacrament is God placing Jesus Christ into the present moment of the believer in tangible form. As the Psalm says, "*O taste and see that the Lord is good.*" That's what sacraments are all about.

Luther was convinced that by this definition, all church sacraments (Jesus in tangible form for our salvation) had to be:

a) based on a scriptural event with Jesus involved
b) connected to an earthly element
c) based on a promise from God

So, he pared them down to just two: Baptism and Holy Communion. I see, in my imagination, Luther agonizing over shrinking the list of seven to the Lutheran list of two. Did you know that Luther almost said that marriage was a sacrament? That's how carefully Luther pared down the list. He worked from the Bible and wanted to prayerfully express what we need when we come to church, not just what we want.

It is what a life of living with the sacraments gives us power to do. Remember again—sacraments give life and salvation by the power and participation of Jesus Christ. They link us to the past, yank us into the here and now, and promise the future. Baptism washes away sin. All the sins. Each day, not just one time. We drown to sin. We rise to new life. If you still wonder how this works, just think of something really skunky that you have done, and how you yearned to turn it back. Being a baptized person does that automatically. If you know it does that, so much the better.

And then, holy communion. You did that skunky thing, that sinful thing, and people found out. Or maybe they didn't. Either way, you felt like you didn't belong anymore. If they knew the real you, they wouldn't want you. You would be out of the running, out of the family, out of the group. One strike, and you're out. That's the best you could hope for. Then, without you imagining it could be true, Jesus came himself and broke bread with you. And shared a glass of wine. His body. His blood.

Suddenly and forever, you, the big sinner, knowing what you'd done, found yourself kneeling next to another big sinner. Suddenly you would all be the same. Jesus and his meal of body and blood would be the only important thing. You would *both* be forgiven, accepted, counted in, and nourished as in no other place.

Those are the sacraments. They have the power to give life. To fill the heart. To give peace everlasting. Someday I'll tell you why I say "come, Lord Jesus" when I drink from the cup. It's not important now, except to know that He will come. He must come. He has come. He will again, finally.

Jesus was twelve years old. He was a good boy. The writing from Luke says that he never disobeyed again. But he did, this once. And he had fun. Here's what he was doing. He was learning from the wisest, and teaching from his heart.

Could you do that? That's the part that I sometimes find missing from what Lutherans call, a sacramental life. Learning from the wisest and passing on what you know. Not in a preachy way, but in a way that informs your actions, your kindnesses, your energy, your prayers. Study with others is a big part of the faith. Without it, you are only relying on half a faith. With it, you are as strong as Jesus. Well, almost.

Oh, and yes. At the end of the garage sale at the Roman Catholic college, someone noticed that I was looking for something. They brought out a Roman Catholic missal, like the altar book that we work from every week to lead worship. It was bound in red leather, and was all in Latin, with engravings of Jesus and the other leaders of the faith. It was printed in France, in 1937. I was offered to take it home for a nominal fee. Of course, I did.

Every time I look at it, I think of the old lady in red lipstick looking for her copy of that famous novel. She was looking for one thing, and like me, God was preparing to send her another.

A life of learning and sharing what you know about God, fueled and anchored by baptism and Holy Communion, sends her, and many like her, and even you and me, what God wants us to have. It is salvation. It is life. It is ours.

11

EPIPHANY: FOLLOW YOUR STAR

Matthew 2:10–11

> *When they saw that the star had stopped, they were*
> *overwhelmed with joy. On entering the house, they saw the*
> *child with Mary his mother; and they knelt down and paid*
> *him homage.*

> *Heavenly Father, it's time to greet king Jesus with little gifts, then pay*
> *homage to him.*
> *What gifts would he want? What could he use? The shopping list is*
> *short. He'll take our hearts, wrapped in love for him. In Christ's name*
> *we pray. Amen*

Epiphany is the celebration of Christ being made known.
As knowing about Jesus spreads out from Bethlehem into
the world, some strange things happen. King Herod thinks
of murder.

The magi, the three kings, the wise men think of what it would be
like to bend those old, out-of-practice knees to this new king. Strange
things happen when Christ is made known.

Here's a strange one. When my son was a boy, he was a Boy Scout. That involved pinewood derbies, weekend campouts, tying knots, and merit badges. It also involved meetings of Boy Scouts in dens on weeknights, and "please remember to pick up a gallon of milk when you pick up your son at the Boy Scout meeting on your way home" requests from your wife.

That's why we were standing in front of the milk counter in the grocery store one weeknight when a woman approached us. Short, with a slight frame, she was shaking.

She was dressed up, which is to say dressed modestly, like for church. She had prepared words of introduction.

"I see that your son is in scouting. I like his uniform. He looks very handsome in it. If you're in scouting, you must have a very strong system of values. That's how I know you would be interested in my church." She then offered the name of her congregation, directions, and service times. Then, still shaking, she stood there silently. It occurred to me that she had never gotten this far with anyone before. She didn't know what to do and neither did we.

There were certain things going on here that had to be acknowledged. One was the bravery, if misguided, of the young woman standing next to us. Another was my son's ideas about what would happen to you if you actually invited someone to church. So, I thanked the lady for asking us to church and said we had a very fine church of our own.

At that, she actually ran down the grocery aisle and headed for the door. Poor thing. For a minute I was mad at her church, whatever it was, for making her do something that was obviously scaring her senseless.

Do you get angry when you think about Epiphany? I'll bet not. At least it doesn't occur to you that Epiphany is what makes you angry. But no matter what name you put to it, sooner or later every good Christian gets angry, whether it's at the pastor's urging to be better evangelists or … at Epiphany. That's one of the strange things that happen when it's time for Christ to be made known. We get a little angry.

Let me tell you why I think that happens.

For Matthew, everything about Jesus and his birth reminded him of Moses.

The magi were like the ancient magicians who challenged Moses as an adult. Moses won. God wins. God is the only real power. This makes the magi in Jesus' story happy, gladdening their hearts.

It doesn't make King Herod happy, though. In the Moses story, the Egyptian pharaoh sends out an order to kill all the Hebrew children, including baby Moses. Herod does the same thing. It seems like with Moses and with Jesus, everybody knows about these newborn babies and how they bring God into the world. You just never know who's going to get mad and who's going to be happy with this information.

Herod and the pharaoh get mad. Magi and shepherds, sheep and oxen are glad. How do you feel about the prospect of making Christ known in the world?

Here's a checklist to help you decide.

How do you feel about bended knees? What that means is worship, and it means worship in all the gospels. And worship in the gospels is actually very simple. It means making yourself lower than God and enjoying it.

Once when I was in a big community choir that performed choral arrangements from Broadway musicals, I had to spend the first ten minutes on bended knee, front and center with about ten other guys, while we sang "The Phantom of the Opera." I thought, this is dumb. Then my knees started to hurt, and I thought some other choice thoughts. "The Phantom of the Opera" is not good enough to bend my knee for ten minutes.

If the thought of making Christ known strikes you as dumb, inconvenient, painful, or just unnecessary, then maybe it's time to rethink what *your* opinion is of the person you are bending your knee for, the Christ.

How do you feel about welcoming strangers? That's what the magi were doing, after all.

Jesus, as an infant, was a stranger in a strange land. The gifts they brought him seemed a little wacked out. Gold for a baby. Not bad. Frankincense. That'll smell up the nursery, but it's really for worship. Myrrh. A chemical for treating a dead body for burial. Jesus' death is so much a part of his life, even from the start. What gifts would we give him now?

Hospitality to those who visit us. Christ is made known when we welcome the stranger. Are you capable of doing a mission trip, to help people in another country, say, and show them God cares? It's possible. Has anyone gotten your specific prayers lately? Prayers from you are a gift, as well. Offer your good gifts, to make Christ known.

Here's another thought. The magi followed a star, through the night sky. Please don't bore me with conjectures and calibrations about whether or not a real star was in that ancient sky. That's not the point. The point is that the magi transformed their lives by following a calling from God that looked like a star in the sky. They were following a calling from God. That's how they made Christ known.

Ask yourself, right now, what is God calling you to do, to move on, to follow him, to get going for His sake? No answer? Keep asking. Got an answer? Test it out to make sure it's real. If you can find two or three other people to help, to work it through together, to give your calling legs, then it's almost certainly something like that star in the sky for the magi. What's your calling?

Some may refer to that calling, following that star by the word "discipleship." You are a disciple, made to follow a star that's sent from God.

In that grocery store, there was a Boy Scout, a dad, and a lady terrified of making Christ known. Aren't we all? Relax. Most of what we know about Christ is made known by people who simply follow their star go where God guides them, and get others to go with them.

They are disciples. You are one of them. Bend the knee. Then, look up to find your star.

12
REACTIVE/RESPONSIVE

Matthew 2:1–4

In the time of King Herod, after Jesus was born in Bethlehem of Judea, wise men from the East came to Jerusalem, asking, "Where is the child who has been born king of the Jews? For we observed his star at its rising and have come to pay him homage." When King Herod heard this, he was frightened, and all Jerusalem with him; and calling together all the chief priests and scribes of the people, he inquired of them where the Messiah was to be born.

Lord Christ, King Herod was out of control. He wasn't the only one. Forgive us when we lash out in anger or fear like he did, no matter how big or small the results. Then, like the Wise Men, lead us once more to behold the gentility and grace of your presence. Amen.

Epiphany used to be one of the three big days of the church year. The other ones were Easter and Pentecost. This was, of course, before the Macy's Thanksgiving Parade and a host of other diversions. But it could be one of the big three again. Epiphany means "making Christ known." Just how you manage that, and you do, is always a delightful surprise.

I began to notice that I was probably being called by God to the ordained ministry when I was a senior in high school. What, may I ask even at this late date, was God thinking? I was tall, awkward, and painfully shy— just right for making Christ known. (That was sarcasm). But God wasn't being sarcastic at all. He had something in mind. He does these things all the time. You probably know more about it than I do. God's calling to make Christ known.

Thanks to the school system's then-rabid focusing on students making a career choice, sometime right after kindergarten, my high school senior friends used to ask me what I was going to be after college.

There were the friends that I parked next to in the school parking lot. Easy to find any morning. Brother and sister, they were big and tough and drove a super-annuated Ford Thunderbird. They were my friends. They were worried about gas mileage and whether anyone was bothering me (they'd gladly beat them up). They were not worried about their calling from God. Maybe, just maybe, they already had that under control. Could be.

But not me. I would hesitantly announce to others, less earthy and secure, that I was thinking about becoming a pastor. Sure. Right. And just how do you plan to tell people about Christ? Slip them a note, unsigned? That was a thought.

One day, during a break of some kind at school, a guy I knew sat me down and said, "Tell me about all this pastor stuff." I should have known better. Having heard what I had to say, he offered his own take. He said something like, "In our church, we don't have any pastors. The New Testament says that every one of us is an evangelist. Go ahead, then. Show me where in the Bible it said that we need to pay a pastor to have a church."

Well, he had me. Not necessarily because he was right, but because at that point my religious education was deplorable.

So, when I joined the Lutheran church, I remembered how my high school "friend" had let me know how I would be as a pastor.

Unnecessary. I could have, with some knowledge and religious training, *responded*. That would have meant I had something to say about myself that defined who I was and what I wanted to do.

A *response* always says something positive about you. It does not attack the other person to make a point, or make you feel better. That would be a *reaction*. A reaction begins when something someone says or does, strikes fear in your heart, and you find a way to defend yourself. Sarcasm has almost always been my weapon of choice.

But, when I was younger, and new as a Lutheran (1971), I chose liturgical purity. With my nose firmly planted in midair, I would disdain anyone and everyone who violated the clear-cut, if arcane, rules of liturgy. This hymn is good, that one bad. Here's why. Rock music in church is bad, and I can prove it theologically. I gathered a little group of friends around me who thought the same way. We were happy, but we were insufferable.

Always reactive, we were on the lookout all the time for impurities and mistakes in worship. We went to worship at another church once, and because the pastor was wearing vestments incorrectly, we howled with derisive laughter. We were also cowards. Reactivity can make a person a coward. That would be a person who acts brave, but out of fear or anger (or both at once) puts any opponent under the gun.

I've done it many times. Reactive Richard. What a pity. Wasted years. But make no mistake, it is fun being right. That's why it's easy to stay reactive for so long.

This problem is larger than we might imagine. *Responsive vs. reactive.* In the post-Christmas world, King Herod was reactive. He heard about a newborn king, the messiah from God. "King? I'm king. Only me. No other. So, I'll trick the wise men into telling me where this infant king can be found (so that I too may worship him, ha, ha!) and then I'll have him killed." That plan didn't work. So, he ordered all the newborns in the general area to be killed. There. Reaction noted. King Herod safe.

Now, that's reactivity. But there's more. Not only was King Herod afraid of the little king, but the whole of Jerusalem was in a fearful uproar as well. How can this happen? I thought the people of God were supposed to be *living* for the coming of the messiah. Instead, they want to kill him dead. Eventually, they do.

I guess that things ossify after a while. They grow dead and brittle. You have your temple, and your worship practices, and your other accoutrements, and after a time anyone who seeks to change them is the enemy. I can understand that because I've done it, too. But that doesn't make it right. Then, fearful to the max, you strike out at anyone who seems to oppose you. Little king, messiah from God? Kill him dead. And don't let any grass grow under your feet.

I like the *response, not reaction* of the wise men better. If only I could copy them a little more consistently. They are Zoroastrians, of course. That means that they follow the teachings of Zoroaster, not Zorro. They study religion. They study the stars in the night sky. The stars are telling them that a messiah of some kind has been born in parts west. Better go check it out, and if true, worship him.

How can Zoroastrianism get people to Jesus? Don't ask me. Because, when I get that news, I feel defensive and unsure. Only Christians bring Jesus to people. Oh really?

Ask the wise men about that. God seems to be bigger than what we know. And we know plenty. We know the creeds, which are the Spirit-inspired summary of the cosmic work of God. We know Christmas, which is the birth in human form of a formerly remote God, now among us, and in a way, one of us. This produces in us something called love. And love begins to allow for God to move in all directions.

As I say, this all comes from the response of the wise men. No idiots, they saw through the reactive King Herod right away. They made their excuses and got away from him. How do you handle reactive people around you? Do you fall into their insecurity, and the need for everyone to feel the same way? Or do you stay open to what God is doing around you?

When you are telling everyone that you think God is calling you to the ordained ministry, the church gets involved. They have a million questions to separate the ones who are mistaken from the ones who have an actual calling. I found a loophole. (That was sarcasm).

Once in seminary, I was still under the power of my high school friend who didn't think much of pastors. I was still reactive. Then, God started throwing me curve balls, just for the fun of it, I think.

One time, I was showing my friends around the big cathedral near the seminary. It was dark inside. Incense was still wafting around inside from the last worship service. Priests were in the confessional, hearing about the need of believers for forgiveness. As a Lutheran, (brand name, protected by patent), I thought I should probably be put off by this high-churchy display.

Then, from nowhere, out of the shadows, a small woman appeared. Draped with shawls and other indeterminate garb, she got into my face and handed me a rosary. She said, "At heart, you are a nice boy. I know. I can tell. Pray the rosary every day, will you? That way, people may come to know the Virgin Mary and her son, Jesus."

Huh? What? My response, as you've probably already sensed, was highly reactive. I wanted to run, or to debate her down to a quivering mass. Lutheran, not Catholic! I would win, I knew it.

So reactive. Fight or flight. Hurt your opponent or run away. But, our Epiphany work is to leave reactivity behind, and become responsive. I took the rosary she had to offer. Because the experience was so different, it seemed to sting in my hand. But she was doing something that I couldn't yet do, for all my theological education. She was responding to the call of Jesus the Messiah to make his name known. I took the rosary. And I took something else with me.

Epiphany is making Christ known. A Zoroastrian star, a traveling wise man with presents of gold, or frankincense, or myrrh, or a lady of the shadows with rosaries and prayer advice … all the same. They are Epiphany. Making Christ known. You don't have to be perfect, theologically or otherwise. You just have to know the difference between being reactive and being responsive, open, listening, and giving what you have. That's all it takes.

Epiphany.

13
New Names

John 1:29

Here is the Lamb of God who takes away the sins of the world.

Father in Heaven, it sounds like everybody gets a new name. Jesus is called the Lamb of God. Cephas is called Peter, the rock. Maybe you have a new name for us, one that tells us what you want us to be. Quiet ... we are listening for your name for us, and what you are calling us to be. In Christ's name we pray. Amen.

Our son was a toddler when we first started thinking about the Fourth of July parade in our rural Illinois town. Our nanny, the woman who took care of our son while we were working, gave us the idea. The weekly newspaper had a contest every year for the best Fourth of July costume. We entered our two-year-old son.

I'm not sure what an appropriate patriotic costume for a toddler could be, but whatever it was, we won. The next year, we tried even harder to create the perfect costume, and won again. The first prize was a red ribbon, a little medallion, and five dollars. Our son was beginning to collect these. They were mounted on the wall of his room.

By the time he reached the age of four, the demands on our imagination were tremendous. What costume and float would win? How could we top last year? For his fourth entry in the parade, he was Ben Franklin, complete with vest, rectangular glasses made with pipe cleaners, and a liberty bell on the red wagon in back of him.

He won again.

That night, after the fireworks, there was a family conference. We decided that it was time to let someone else win the Fourth of July Parade competition. Our son would step aside, his winning streak a thing of the past. The following summer, a little girl dressed up as Betsy Ross was the winner. It was hard for him to let go of his old identity as the winner, but we made it work. I guess you could say it was a part of our son's maturity to move on and find a new way of thinking about himself. Maybe that was the year he started preschool, going off for the first time.

One thing I do know, the gospel in John chapter 1 is calling us out of what we once were, and into what God calls us to be.

John the Baptist, on a winning streak with water and the Jordan River, had called a nation to leave behind their self-satisfaction—I believe the word he used was "repent"—and try a new way of following God.

Out of all that water, John got a clear sense that something bigger was coming. It was Jesus. He was the Messiah, the savior. John had as strong a sense of that as we did the night we decided not to enter the parade contest again. It was time for something new.

Time to grow, to mature. When John saw Jesus walking along, and the moment was right, John could say, "Look, there goes the Lamb of God." Part of the maturing process that was happening to John was letting go of his past overwhelming success with water—baptizing—and pointing to Jesus. He even gave Jesus a new name, *Lamb of God*.

From now on, let's call John's maturing process, *God's calling*. Let's also say that, according to John's gospel and what he is telling us, is that life with Jesus also means being *called* and it means getting a new name.

In fact, the next thing that happens is that Andrew hears John give Jesus his new name and his new calling, to be the Lamb or sacrifice for our sins. Then, Andrew gets his brother, Cephas, to come and meet Jesus. I'm looking for a pattern here, and I'm not disappointed. The same thing happens again: new calling, leaving the old behind, and new name. This time, Cephas the brother of Andrew, becomes *Peter, the Rock*.

It will be a long time before anyone could be less like a rock than Peter. He tries to walk on water like Jesus, and he sinks. He tries to give Jesus his new and permanent name, *Messiah*, and he misses the meaning. Jesus doesn't care about any of that. Not really.

Jesus calls Peter to follow him and gives Peter the new name that will gradually fit him.

Now, as far as I can tell, one of the main reasons John's gospel tells us all this is to show us a pattern. John turns from the water, names the lamb, and then Jesus turns from John and names the rock, the man who will be the rock of the new church later on. Every time a new name is named, a new calling happens.

It happens all over the Bible. Abram is asked to follow God, and God calls him *Abraham*. His wife, Sarai, also gets a new name, *Sarah*.

Jacob stays up all night wrestling with God, to see who has the stronger will. When morning comes, Jacob gets a new name, *Israel*, which means to struggle with God.

Now, it's nice to find patterns in the Bible, but what does it mean? Since we know that God likes repeating this pattern, what it probably means is that sooner or later *you* are going to get a new name, and a new calling. Words like maturing, following, growing in faith all describe this. But the simplest way to say it is that sooner or later, you are going to be part of this pattern, of being called and getting a new name.

One thing I haven't told you about the little church I served where the Fourth of July Parade was, is that the people in the church couldn't bring themselves to call me by any name. Their other pastor had been there for twenty-three years, and they weren't about to call anyone else pastor without a good reason. And maybe not even then. I think it took them about three years. And it happened in the strangest possible way. And it was also part of the pattern, being called to follow Jesus, then getting the name.

Before I came to that church, four young people joined. They were fun and full of energy, and they were also quadriplegics, meaning that they had no use of either their arms or legs, and were confined to wheelchairs. Members of the congregation were always needed to hold their hymnals during worship and have a spare Kleenex on hand for a momentary drool or a grateful tear. It was clear that the congregation was being called to do whatever we could for these four young people, but the truth was that no one was overly willing, including me.

Then one of the four got an idea. His name was Harold. The Memorial Day parade was coming up, and Harold had a vision. The four quadriplegics could be on a float with the church's name on the sides. I had practical arguments about how this would not work, but Harold didn't give up. He said, "When people see us on the float, they will know that God loves everyone, and can work in everyone's life. We have to show them that God is a God of power and grace." Try arguing with that.

When someone offered us a spare float for free, and I found a driver with a Suburban and a trailer hitch, Harold's float was a done deal. When the parade was over, Harold was the last of the four we lifted off the float. As the wheels of his wheelchair touched the pavement, he said, "Thank you, Pastor Dow."

"What did you say?"

"I said, thank you, Pastor Dow.'"

"Harold," I said, "that's the first time a member of this congregation has used my name."

Simple, isn't it? It fits a pattern. The new name went along with my calling to tell people what our church stood for. They go together. Not too many people in our little congregation liked being represented by a bunch of quadriplegics in the parade. I know, because they told me so. But when they did, they called me Pastor Dow. For the first time! It was exciting, at last, to have a calling, and a new name.

Think about this. No, pray about it. What is it, right now, that God is calling you to do in your faith? And, to go with that calling, what is *your* new name?

14

WATER INTO WINE AND OTHER ASSORTED MIRACLES

John 2:1–5

> *On the third day there was a wedding in Cana of Galilee, and the mother of Jesus was there. Jesus and his disciples had also been invited to the wedding. When the wine gave out, the mother of Jesus said to him, "They have no wine." And Jesus said to her, "Woman, what concern is that to you and to me? My hour has not yet come." His mother said to the servants, "Do whatever he tells you."*

Lord Jesus, we panic when things don't go as we think they should. Panic. We forget who is truly in charge. We forget to expect the miracle. Restore peace to our hearts and belief to our tired spirits. Amen.

You know the story of Rumpelstiltskin. (But just don't say his name.)

But he's the only one in the story who has a name.

There is a dad who is hoping to become a big deal in town. So, he tells a false tale about his daughter. Listen up. She can turn straw into gold. Over this false fact, everyone goes crazy. Even the king is not immune to a lie that's big enough. He sends for the girl and locks her in a room. Her task is to live up to her publicity. But she can no more turn straw into gold than she can turn water into wine. Oops. I'm getting ahead of myself.

Taking a "straw poll," for what else is there in her little cell, the girl decides that she is in deep trouble. She is liable to lose her head over this one. Then, poof, Rumpel-you-know-who appears, as if from nowhere. He promises to turn straw into gold and get the girl out of this jam. But everything costs something in this world, doesn't it?

On the first spin, she gives him her necklace. The gold from the straw piles up. Voila! On the second spin, she gives him a bracelet. More gold appears, but it is not enough. On the third spin, something more is required. The rumpled Rumpel-guy names it: her firstborn. The girl thinks, "Buy now, pay later. Let's do it!"

In a couple of fast moves, the girl's life was changed forever. The king married the golden girl, they had a child, and the stilt-and-skin guy demanded payment for services rendered: "Cough up the kid. Unless," he said, in a moment of vanity, "you can guess my name." She did some Googling, found his name just like that, and said it to his face, "Rumpelstiltskin!" Again, poof. He spun himself into the ground, and by all reports stayed there.

Straw into gold, water into wine. What's the difference? There may not be any difference at all. Straw into gold and water into wine. Well, there is one difference, maybe. The water-into-wine miracle and sign from John's gospel is conspicuously lacking a villain. There is no Rumpelstiltskin there. Or is there?

I know another way to say his name. Here goes: Rumpelstiltskin translates nicely into this phrase: Fear that you don't have enough. *Fear that you don't have enough.*

I ran out of money on a college basketball tournament trip once, and it was no fun. Fear that you don't have enough. In a panic, I called my parents and asked for a money order or something. I learned to count my pennies. To this day I get a little feeling of panic when it's time to buy something. Fear, as I say, of not having enough. This fear plays cruel tricks on a person.

This fear-factor may be exactly what the water-into-wine adventure is all about. A mere two thousand years ago, weddings lasted a week. They were about brides and parties, I guess, but they were also about the community, and how God had blessed everybody in it. So, as you may know, running out of wedding wine was an uncomfortable reminder that there might not really be enough of anything. Fear became a guest at the wedding—and things had been going so well.

Enter Jesus. But he's not alone. His mother Mary is with him. In John's gospel, she only makes two appearances with her son, one at this wedding, and one at the cross while he is dying. There are only two outings with Jesus and Mary together, so they must be important.

Here's the part I could never figure out. Mary figures out that the wine supply has run dry. Disastersville ahead. Mary commands Jesus to do something about this lack. Here's where Jesus loses me. He says to his mom, "My hour has not yet come." So, it looks like Jesus is going to insist on some theological sub-point while a disappointed bride, groom, and the whole town go home early, their faith shaken. That just doesn't sound like Jesus.

Chances are, I'm not going to solve that question about Jesus today. Maybe you're ahead of me on this and already know the answer. I do know that there are some clues.

First clue. Mary doesn't get stressed out when wine runs out. Instead, she tells the servants to do what Jesus says. When in doubt, let Jesus have a crack at the problem. See what happens.

Second clue. The wine runs out on the third day. Where else have we seen this three days phenomenon? The third day. The third day was the resurrection of Jesus. See? When you let Jesus loose on a problem, then or now, you face fear and realize a resurrection.

I saw a weird scene in an old movie called *The Big Sleep*. Lauren Bacall was singing to a group of people in a gambling club. Why she was doing this was never made clear. She sang a song called "The Water Flows Like Wine." Get it? The writer of the song knew his or her Bible. But in the Bible, the *wine* flows like *water*. So, was Bacall saying that in real life, it's different, and that what we get is only water? Better learn to make do. I guess that's movie logic for you. Cynical, isn't it?

Are churches equally cynical? Water into wine? Or straw into gold? Is our faith equally cynical? Time to call out Rumpelstiltskin by his real name. Fear. Fear that God won't give us enough. Fear that asks for cutbacks and compromises. Name your fear, and just maybe it will spin itself into the ground. Maybe. Still cynical?

I hope that I haven't worn this story out with the telling, but I think things are more powerful when you see them with your own eyes.

My church in Dallas was having financial problems. Budgets had already been cut to the bone. People were afraid. I was afraid. I had been taught, and would be taught again, that when God asks you to do something (like serve wine through the whole wedding, or pay the bills while raising a family, or run a church like Christ would like it to run), then God provides what you need to get it done.

The small congregation I was serving had the usual experience of low summer offerings. They had always gotten through this fallow period before, but this year was different. When people talk about their fears with the language of faith (and this was a real one), Jesus can and will show us ways to move beyond them. This congregation was good at that, but not this time. Instead, there was talk about drastic cuts for staff salaries, and other cuts that would end basic programs. It felt exciting for them to answer fear with negativity, as it always does. My "water into wine" task was to respond as well, but without the fear.

I called a special council meeting. I explained in every way I could that I was not going to respond to the problem with fear, and that they had some big decisions to make about their future.

Then the council called several meetings to revise the budget. What they did next completely surprised me. They decided to *add* to the budget where they felt God's call to ministry was underfunded. They maintained, but did not increase my salary, because it was not warranted. They passed the new budget unanimously.

Then they did another thing that surprised me. That summer, when offerings were always perilously low, each Sunday's offerings were just a little more than what we needed to get ministry moving and keep it moving.

Straw into gold? Water into wine? Really? Once in a while it's time for people in churches to do what the water-into-wine story asks us to do. First, to ask ourselves what our greatest fear is. Go ahead. Close your eyes for a moment. Honestly, and silently, what is your greatest fear here? Open your eyes. We might start talking among each other over coffee or over prayer about what those fears are. Sometimes, we are tempted to simply ask other people to take on those fears by talking about what they did wrong. That has no place among us now.

So then, secondly, what do you believe a good, solid third-day resurrection experience for us would be like? Some of us will think, how about more wine? Instead, close your eyes. Imagine what God could do among us. Let your imagining turn to prayer, and your prayer to strength for action.

Open your eyes. Straw into gold? Water into wine? Perhaps it's about time.

15
Dialing Up a New Me

Luke 4:14–21

Then Jesus, filled with the power of the Spirit, returned to Galilee, and a report about him spread through all the surrounding country. He began to teach in their synagogues and was praised by everyone. When he came to Nazareth, where he had been brought up, he went to the synagogue on the Sabbath day, as was his custom. He stood up to read, and the scroll of the prophet Isaiah was given to him. He unrolled the scroll and found the place where it was written: "The Spirit of the Lord is upon me, because he has anointed me to bring good news to the poor. He has sent me to proclaim release to the captives and recovery of sight to the blind, to let the oppressed go free, to proclaim the year of the Lord's favor." And he rolled up the scroll, gave it back to the attendant, and sat down. The eyes of all in the synagogue were fixed on him. Then he began to say to them, "Today this scripture has been fulfilled in your hearing."

Lord Jesus, you come up with some bold words to start up your ministry, your work. What's the boldest word I could come up with to get my ministry going in your name? Help me to phrase it, Lord. In your holy name we pray. Amen.

When my parents were ill, I would fly across country to see them every other month, taking turns with my sister. When we prepared them for the move to Florida and cleared out their house, my friends volunteered their parents' home, now vacant, for me to stay in.

The guest room where I stayed had a sleep number bed. That is a kind of bed where you get to dial your own personal number for your sleepy-time comfort. The commercial says that because you are an individual, you need a mattress that adjusts to your individuality. In that case, I am in deep trouble.

Every night, I would dial a number that I thought more or less matched my extreme individuality. Then, assured that the universe was carefully attuned to my needs, I would fall asleep. The morning after would bring a rotten little surprise. The sleep number mattress had responded to my individual needs by completely deflating. So much for my individual personality. Or, perhaps the beginning.

For the Christian, this is a part of a process. First, there is the deflating of my own puffed-up—or dialed-up—sense of who and what I am in this world, if only while asleep. It works better if you are awake. The second part of the process is dialing up a new and better me. You know, like Jesus did when he started his ministry.

Jesus does all this and more during a sermon in his home town, Nazareth. It seems like he's been preparing for this little talk for a long time. It deflates a lot of things, but it's meant to fill up our hearts, possibly with the Holy Spirit, if we allow it. Jesus allowed it. Maybe he even welcomed it. What do you think?

Jesus goes back to the prophet Isaiah—way back, as a matter of fact. Back to the time when the people of God were exiled from their land for a persistently unfaithful game plan, personally and nationally. Then, God brought them back home. In the midst of this historic "time out," God had some startling things to say about being a child of God. They were unique, and were supposed to form a new identity, personally and nationally. The time for sleep was over. Time to wake up to a new way of living.

What, you may be wondering, was this new way? I think you've guessed it. It's the way of the servant, and what Jesus, as both servant and King will do. The people of God have a way of suppressing this, and God has a way of bringing it up again.

Jesus writes his sermon. Or maybe it's so much a part of him that he just thinks it through during a long walk or something. It rings true because it is true. Isaiah nailed it, so Jesus uses his words: to bring good news to the poor; to proclaim release to the captives; recovery of sight to the blind; to let the oppressed go free; to proclaim the year of the Lord's favor.

Then, Jesus rolled up the scroll containing those words, and he sat down. That's all that needed to be said. Jesus has nailed his identity for sure. And, if we want, gives us our identity anew.

The thing is, Jesus had help writing this sermon. His mom helped him. Remember when she found out she was pregnant she sang a song that's called "The Magnificat."

Here it is, at least part of it.

"My soul magnifies the Lord and my spirit rejoices in God my Savior, for he has looked with favor on the lowliness of his servant. Surely, from now on all generations will call me blessed; for the Mighty One has done great things for me, and holy is his name. His mercy is for those who fear him from generation to generation. He has shown strength with his arm; he has scattered the proud in the thoughts of their hearts. He has brought down the powerful from their thrones and lifted up the lowly; he has filled the hungry with good things and sent the rich away empty."

Mary was probably like the rest of us. Maybe, like us, she liked to sing her child to sleep at night. When I reach into the back of my mind for something, I used to sing to our children, I usually come up with a Broadway show tune. I guess I was lucky my kids didn't grow up to be Ethel Merman. Mary sang her Magnificat to Jesus. It was her way of looking at the world. It was her way of understanding God. And, so singing, she was giving her son an understanding of who he was. She was giving him an understanding of what God was all about … in him. And, in us, under certain circumstances.

My concern is that this jaw-dropping moment in Jesus' life and ministry are not repeated in too many pulpits anymore. Neither are they repeated in too many lives. Why not? Too busy dialing up our personal sleep numbers? And do most sermons, including some of my own, encourage that personal spiritual sleepy-time experience? Probably so. It seems to me that any talk about being Christian without connecting it to others in need falls as flat as my little sleep number bed. And it should.

Instead, the words of Jesus to proclaim good news to the broken and captive, the hungry and hopeless, must keep running like a thread through the history of God's people. Right up to now.

When I look for it, here's what I see.

Two friends and I found ourselves walking up the unyielding granite steps of a federal courthouse. The climb wasn't easy because we knew what we were facing. We were there to support a mother and son, in deep trouble, the son accused of crimes that, if proven, would ruin his life. The son was petrified. The mom was bitter at the accusation.

The prosecution presented their case while we sat in the back of the courtroom. The mom and son knew we were there. That was important. I didn't know how important until they spoke with us afterward, overflowing with thanksgiving that they were not alone.

On the other side of the world, in Haiti, missionaries from a Lutheran seminary were present during the 2010 earthquake. You probably saw the news. Maybe you also heard about the missionaries, and what became of them.

One young man was trapped in the wreckage of the Lutheran House, while his wife and friends came as close to him as they dared, fearing for their own safety. They could not see him, but knew he was not going to survive. They heard his resonant voice sing hymn after hymn, giving glory to God until the wreckage pressed inward and his breath gave out. I thought, I don't even know any hymns well enough to sing them by myself.

What is there about this event that makes my jaw drop and sends me to my knees? Is it from Mary's song to Jesus' sermon, to hymns in the wreckage from a dying singer? What's happening here?

Meanwhile, returning to the courtroom and our friend, there was an acquittal for her son, and rejoicing in the halls of the federal courthouse. The following year, the mom joined other Christians on a missionary trip to Haiti. The bitterness in her heart long ago been replaced by reverence and joy. What kind of missionary work would she do there, for a land overwhelmed by an earthquake, two hurricanes, a million homeless, and widespread cholera?

I'm not sure, exactly. But I know that from many decades of ministry where I've never gone without food, electricity, or a shower, that God may be dialing down that self-centered identity and letting me know that God has my number, too. I am and always have been a child of God, a servant of the servant God, and his people. But, you heard Jesus' sermon too. Did your jaw drop a little, and did you fall to your knees? Then, now, rise to serve. There are people waiting, yearning for the news you have to give.

16
Blessings and Curses

Luke 6:31

Do unto others as you would have done unto you.

God, you are asking me to be nice to horrible people, and to put myself in harm's way to be generous and kind. I don't like this suggestion, until I remember that you thought you were doing the same thing the last time you forgave me, when you did it from your son's cross. Now it's a little easier to be a little kinder. Thanks for the reminder. In Christ's name, Amen.

What can I tell you about Norm? He worked for my father many years ago as a factory manager. Norm had two rules about his job. The first rule was that he was indispensable. The second rule was that no one else should have any authority.

In a way, this worked well. He was very conscientious about his job, and no detail ever went unaddressed.

This is where I had my initial run-in with Norm. I went to work for my father in the late 1960s, when I was in college. I cleaned the offices and also did some paperwork in the office during the week.

One Saturday I drove to the office early, let myself in, and cleaned. Then, I switched hats and sat at my desk to clear up some paperwork that had been piling up.

I was almost done when there was a knock on the door. It was the driver of a huge semi-trailer truck. The driver explained that inside the truck was a big display from the factory that we had ordered months ago for a special trade show that was coming up. I didn't feel that I had the authority to sign for it, so I called my father at home. He was nowhere to be found.

Then I called Norm, thinking that he could at least give me permission to sign for this important shipment. Norm was out playing golf. Have you ever heard the expression, "Who's minding the store?" Well, that Saturday morning, it was me.

I signed for the display, and several hours later it was on the loading dock, and the semi-driver was on his way. I congratulated myself for a job well done.

But I had forgotten about Norm. Monday morning, Norm sensed that his authority and power had been usurped. I had gone around him. It was treason. He gave me a lecture that I will never forget, humiliating me in front of other workers for taking matters into my own hands. When he was through, my face was red, and I was truly angry. I wanted to tell Norm off in no uncertain terms, and I felt I had a right to.

But I didn't. You see, I had just become a member of the Lutheran church. I joined about a week after I graduated from high school. I had learned Christian ideas like turning the other cheek and blessed are the meek and persecuted when I was a child in Sunday School, but now, because I had stepped forward and joined a church that my family didn't go to, these things seemed to take on a new significance.

In fact, I remember my father saying that he would only get interested in my church life and the church I had joined when it really started to make a difference in my life.

Now, with Norm, was my chance. He was clearly in the wrong, and he was using his job position to make me squirm for taking on some responsibility and initiative that he felt only belonged to him. Stupid Norm, I thought to myself. What if I had let that important shipment go? Where would we be then? I knew I was right. Right?

But then along comes Jesus, with his words for just such an occasion. The people that Jesus blesses are the ones that are humble, meek, and caring. He seems to reserve a special blessing for people who take unkind words for doing what was right, and then don't fight back. I had some feelings about Jesus at that point, and how he had worked hard to tailor his words, called the Beatitudes, just for me. You may have occasionally had that same feeling.

Much worse, Jesus goes on to say that the people who have things figured out to work only to their advantage in this life are cursed. Please remember, a curse from the mouth of Jesus has the full power of the law of God stopping us in our tracks.

It was time for me to come down off the fence as a Christian. Should I let Norm have it, telling him how right I was, and how I had protected myself by calling everyone I could think of before I signed for the stuff? Or should I let my pride take a back seat to this guy, and see if Jesus would bless it in some way?

Sometimes, with the Beatitudes, the blessings for being meek and faithful, and the curses for being proud and powerful, have to be tried out to really understand them.

I tried them out. Bring on the blessings, Jesus. I'll be as meek as I can.

Result? Nothing happened. Life went on as it had on every other day, and as the days became weeks since my decision to go with Jesus' blessed behaviors, nothing much changed. Where were those blessings? I was sure that I would have to sign for another delivery soon, except that this one would be from God, my rich rewards for being nice.

Then, the weeks turned into months, then into years. I stayed on at my father's office.

They found someone else to do the cleaning, which was probably a blessing to everyone.

I graduated to keeping certain reports, filing invoices, following up on backorders and even posting orders in the days before computerized inventory control. There were a lot more Saturdays that I let myself into the office to catch up on work, but where were the blessings?

They never came. Can you imagine?

As I was wondering what Jesus was talking about—"blessed are those who … "—some things started happening that I was scarcely aware of.

Norm gradually stopped being a superannuated ogre and started being a human being.

I would stay after the five o'clock bell (and you can bet Norm always did), and I began to know him. Pretty soon, I knew that he was very active in his church. I found out that he had funded and organized mission trips to South America. I also found out that the same annoying qualities that got my goat at work had made his church life successful. I still don't understand that part, but there you are.

What I do understand now is that one day, long ago, Jesus reached out to me with some words about being blessed, and being cursed, that I scarcely understood. The meek inherit the earth. The person who turns the other cheek did it the right way. The person who always wants to get some clear advantage for himself out of each situation might be wrong. I didn't understand those things, but I knew that if my church life was going to mean anything, it had to start with my behavior. So, I voted for humility and waited for the blessings.

Technically, I now see that when Jesus gave us the Beatitudes, his set of blessings and curses, he was painting in quick, small brushstrokes, the picture of his own life and his own cross. Do we like that picture? Is there any way what we see could appeal to us?

Maybe it takes time.

More years passed, and Norm died. I took my wife to the funeral home for the visitation.

I didn't care for the way his wife was totaling up how many people came as a sign of his worth as a human being. It would have been easy to say something, but Norm and I had a bond by then. A certain call to humility.

When I greeted Norm's widow, I told her that I had worked with her husband for many years. There were many memories. He was a good man.

As I held the hand of Norm's wife, it seemed to me that the only reason I could stand there and comfort her was that long ago I had taken the high road, the humbler part, the way of the meek. And in so doing, I had become Norm's friend, without planning it, almost against my will.

I could offer that friendship back to his widow, as she counted mourners and examined the figures to see if her husband had really mattered. I could say that he did matter.

And that was the blessing. God finally delivered it, and I was happy to sign for it and accept it.

It was what I had been waiting for, and what Jesus promised.

A lot is being said and sung about saints today. Quite rightly so. Maybe the real saints are the ones who listen to Jesus' words, take the humbler part even though they've already thought of another, harsher way. They are the ones who wait to take delivery of the blessings that follow. They are the ones who believe that the blessings will come, for being humble, for staying meek, for turning that famous and much slapped cheek.

They are the ones who believe Jesus, that no matter how they'd like to get back at Norm, just once, if they keep faith with Jesus, they will sign off on those blessings.

17
A Glass or a Stone?

Matthew 6:21

For where your treasure is, there your heart will be also.

Dear God, you tell us to take care of our spiritual needs in private and don't be boastful or loud-mouthed about them. Help us to be humble in our daily journey of following you. Amen.

Back in my early ministry, I was asked to fill a position in the synod, which is the governing body of area Lutheran churches. It had been vacated by a very hard driving, successful pastor of a large Chicago church. He wanted to move on to other things, and I had an opportunity to serve the church in its educational department.

After I had said yes to this new position, my predecessor told me the story of his first heart attack. It happened at the retreat center where the national church did their yearly orientation for educational volunteers. He attended, and during one of the sessions, he started feeling sick. You know what the symptoms would be: shortness of breath, tightness across the chest, and a little line of pain going into the shoulder. Sure enough, he was having a heart attack. But he didn't want to leave the retreat; it was too interesting. The presenters were too good to miss.

So, this is what he did. That night, he noticed that there was wine at the little reception before dinner at the retreat center they were gathered at. He did some math. There were two days to go until the retreat was over. Wine thins the blood. If he had one glass of wine after each meal, his blood would stay thin enough, and he could take care of his heart problems after he got home. So, he made an errand of it, taking six glasses of wine to his room, lining them up precisely, as you would medicine, across his windowsill. And, it worked.

When he told me this, he added the additional note that he supposed that everyone at the reception thought he had alcohol troubles. Not so.

He treated his needs in secret, so that the public person that he was could stay active and involved. I thought I understood, although I hope I never have to use his treatment example personally.

And you know, I probably wouldn't, anyway.

I'm just not that disciplined.

As I thought about the person I replaced on the educational team over the next few months, I began to realize that I was walking in the steps of one of the most organized, motivated, and self-disciplined men I had ever known. That was why I looked up to him. But I also realized I was not disciplined enough to follow his treatment for a heart attack.

What I'm thinking about right now is the similarity between my heart attack friend and Jesus. You don't see the correlation? It has something to do with the decision to take care of your needs in private so that you can be an organized, ready-to-go servant in public. That this sort of thing has gone out of style and is beyond the need to mention, still, there it is.

Jesus was once with his disciples in the midst of the circus that religious life had become in first century Judaism. People were praying by standing on soapboxes and shouting. People were paying other people to ring bells before they prayed. The important thing, they all seemed to be saying, was to turn life inside out, doing private things in public and public things (like, integrity, service, and so on) maybe not at all.

My own theory as to what happened to these men, from noble stock, who had reduced their faith to noisy public prayers and gaudy excess, is that at heart they had given up on the core of their faith and all that was left was what was for show. That's a theory. If it's true, then their lives with God were in terrible danger.

Jesus didn't like what they were doing, that's for sure. I think all that stuff made him sad. We know that one time it made him mad, when he cleaned out the temple. But the focus of the gospel story and of Ash Wednesday is how he ministered to the disciples in the midst of spiritual chaos and bankruptcy.

Jesus said, if I can boil it down, that for their own good, the disciples ought to pray in private. They ought to give money to the poor without a show of it. Be spiritual in private. In public, put on a good face, be available for others. That's how a servant would do it, and that's what you are.

Unfortunately, over the years we've decided that God wants us to suffer in silence. That's what this story about spirituality must mean.

It doesn't mean that at all.

It means that Jesus would like us to tend to our spiritual needs away from the public arena, in a focused and dedicated place, where we can line up those six glasses on a well-chosen windowsill and take care of them.

Let's suppose that they are for our nourishment, those six glasses. I know I'm repeating myself, and it won't be the last time. Let's have each glass stand for something that would make your personal Lent mean something.

How about:

- Daily prayer
- Weekly and midweekly worship
- Reading the Bible

- Serving in some way in and outside the church
- Cultivating a spiritual friendship
- And giving of yourself in time, talent, and money.

I like those six glasses. More, I need them badly. Without them, I will die. With them, I can live. They are to be taken in private, here, where worship is well considered and where we are protected and safe, loved and well-known.

Do you object to glasses such as these? There are good reasons. My friend's approach to his heart troubles was flawed, even as it led me into a deeper appreciation of the spirituality that Jesus offers the disciples and me.

How about stones? We have five of those.

Please consider them with me during the weeks of Lent, preceding Easter, as we make our way to the cross and its outcome:

- God's law on a stone, and our hearts.
- The millstone that our sin ties us to.
- The stumbling stone that Jesus is—or is he the rock of salvation?
- Jesus as a living stone, the kind the church grows from.
- And, finally, Jesus the foundation stone, the kind you can build a life on.

From the time Jesus advised the disciples to pray and give quietly, to his own quiet words from the cross that changed the universe, Jesus knew—and understood that we must know, for life, for health, for salvation—that we must care for our hearts in quiet, where we are protected and safe, so that we may meet the challenges and know the joys of our faith in public. It's as simple as a stone, and as solid.

18

Easter Light: Do Not Be Afraid

Matthew 28:5–6

> *But the angel said to the women, "Do not be afraid; I know that you are looking for Jesus who was crucified. He is not here; for he has been raised, as he said. Come, see the place where he lay.*

Dear God, you tell us to take care of our spiritual needs in private and don't be boastful or loud-mouthed about them. Help us to be humble in our daily journey of following you. Amen.

Every year on Easter Sunday, Martin Luther, Lutheran Reformer and parish pastor, used to tell a joke. He said that it was so that his congregation could laugh at the devil and death on the day of Jesus' resurrection. Good reason for a joke.

Enough of death. Enough of human suffering. Enough of sin. We can rejoice in the face of this terrible triumvirate, sin, death, and suffering, because of Jesus and his resurrection from the dead.

This helps us to understand the new world of resurrection and promise that our Lord has created on Easter morning.

I have never completely understood Yad Vashem, the museum dedicated to the Holocaust, the killing of 6 million Jews, which is located outside of Jerusalem, on the promontory of a hill. I had the honor to travel there several years ago with a group of pastors.

Approaching Yad Vashem, the first thing I saw was a box car, one of those used to transport victims to the concentration camps, and their death. It was red and hung cantilevered from the side of a hill. It looked like an idea or a memory, suspended in time and space. If a memory, it prepared me for what I was about to see and experience, suspended in midair, again, like a thought unresolved and unfinished. The boxcar.

At the entrance to the memorial, there was a building, angular, done in white. Tourists are asked not to use flash cameras inside. Here's why. The building was constructed by two Holocaust survivors, husband and wife, who lost their child in the camps, then moved to Los Angeles to make their fortune. Step inside with me.

The first thing you notice is the few candles, lighted and burning. Not much light. Then you notice that the angular walls are all covered with mirrors, reflecting and refracting the light, multiplying it many times. The plaque says that 2 million children were killed in the Holocaust. Your mind begins to add things up, to pull meaning out of things you already know. Two million children. Millions of rays of light reflected from few sources, shining bright. Then, you think of Abraham. God declares to Abraham and Sarah, childless, therefore without hope for the future. God says, *"Your descendants will be more numerous than the stars in the heavens."* Like the light reflected from those few small candle sources.

And, if perhaps you are like me, you think, whatever happened to all those bright promises? What happened to God's promises of good, let loose in the world?

Now leave the children's pavilion with me. When I visited there, I sat on a bench outside, bent over, crying. Because, I guess, I did not feel too much like I was part of the light. What happened to the promises that God let loose on the world so long ago?

Here are some answers. Sin. Indifference. Selfishness. Mob mentality, insecurity with God and immaturity with each other. Lack of self-honesty about spiritual needs. That's what happened.

And, me? Bent over and in tears, sure that I was offering very little light to reflect and refract in this dark world. I would change. Are you still there with me? Do you know what I'm talking about?

Now, Jesus considers his Father's world. It lays in darkness. Sin. Indifference. Mob mentality. Insecurity with God. Immaturity with each other. Lack of self-honesty. This little light of mine? What happened to it?

Jesus considers his father's world. It lays in darkness. He could have gotten angry with us. Sometimes, there was a little anger. But in the main, it was compassion we heard. Healing the blind. Then talking about being free from darkness. He said, "*I am the light of the world.*"

We locked up that light in a dark prison, then the terrible darkness of Golgotha, then the tomb, when we were sure he was lifeless and harmless. There. We let the darkness take care of the light. That's our way.

No wonder the women who loved Jesus looked for him in the dark tomb. It's what we've grown accustomed to. But, Jesus will have none of it. Jesus looks his Father's world over, looks us through and through. There could have been anger about what we've done with the light of God, but what we got was hope, patience, forgiveness, love. We tend to amplify what anger there was. Sounds are always louder in the dark. But that is not Jesus' way.

Instead, he went to the darkest places, tombs, graves, crosses of suffering, and brought the light. That is what he did on Easter Day. Brought the light to darkness.

We now live in the light. Like that museum on a hill, which lays out human darkness and cruelty and its bankrupt spirit but begins to consider it with the light of God's first promise to Abraham. Are you ready for the light? God will reflect and refract it in a million ways. That is what the resurrection is for.

Now here is what happened on Easter Day. The women went to the tomb, found it empty, and met an angel. The appearance of the angel was terrible in its majesty, with an earthquake and flashes of lightening. It is likely that the women at the tomb were being prepared for a new creation, one where light overcomes darkness.

The angel then speaks. "Do not be afraid."

There's more, and the women decide to tell the other disciples. Jesus meets them on the way. He says, "*Do not be afraid*."

OK, I get it. On Easter Day, the message is, do not be afraid. You might attend Easter worship and see something like Yad Vashem, with its story of human cruelty and death, but see lights kindled and reflected countless times. You might attend Easter worship and see whatever it is that you left in that empty tomb. We've been over the list twice. It begins with sin and goes from there. What did *you* leave in the empty tomb? It doesn't matter anymore. Listen now: Do not be afraid. The light of Jesus, now alive forever, the living Son of God, so like us and so like the father; this light shines in you. So, don't be afraid.

Don't be afraid of the past. Human sin and draconian cruelty? You'll see it, when you look into that empty tomb, and your eyes get used to the darkness again. Don't let your eyes get used to the darkness again. Look to Jesus. He lives! He is the light. He is reflected in you. You've got his light in your lives. What will you do with it?

Here's an Easter Story. We are celebrating quietly in our family right now, because of weddings, and because our daughter passed a tough state certification to work with young children. There were three areas of expertise to measure, and she achieved 100 points and more in all areas.

So, how did that story begin? When our daughter was born, the birth process was very difficult. The umbilical cord was wrapped twice around her neck and when she was born, she was purple. I held her first, then they took her away to machines that would support her new life. We held our breaths. The news was, no damage done in any way. However, we weren't sure we believed them. There was oxygen deprivation for a time, but how long? There was slight nerve damage done—very slight—and our beautiful daughter still has a nearly imperceptible drop to one corner of her mouth when she smiles fully.

The years passed, and she started school. She was having some trouble learning. The word came back to us: your daughter has Attention Deficit Disorder. I got a pile of books from the library, and on the way home, I tried to look through them at stoplights. I finally pulled the car over and wept. Didn't the angel and Jesus say, "Do not be afraid?" Of course, they did. It's hard work, though, sometimes.

She had wonderful teachers. Then, I was called to be the pastor of a new church in a different state, one with different educational standards. The first day of class, instead of getting wonderful teachers, my daughter was placed in a class for developmentally disabled children. I was afraid that she would become frightened and give up. I visited the class one day, and she told me with pride that she was helping to teach these wonderful students. Do not be afraid. Show the light of Christ. His resurrection shows anything is possible.

A few more years went by. My daughter found her way into a wonderful class for students like herself, with great imagination, intelligence, and compassionate hearts, who just couldn't concentrate for a long time on any one thing. I talked to the teacher, who was a ball of fire, always energetic, infusing her students with the same energy about getting assignments completed. "You can do it!" she would say, every time.

I asked the teacher how she worked with unfocused students every day, never losing energy. She said something like, "The little darlings. I love each one of them, but I never let up. Jesus is my faith, and I just keep showing 'em the light."

Uh, oh, I thought. Now comes the long religious speech. But, no. The teacher just got back to work. She acknowledged the source of the light. She carried the resurrection with her. It kept her from giving out, or giving up, even once. And now our daughter reflects the light of Christ into the heads and hearts of more children, as a teacher herself.

It's different for everybody, you know. I mean different how you will reflect the light of the risen Christ in the world. Do not, then, let your eyes get too used to the darkness in the empty tomb, which is only a place for the past. Shine Jesus light now. Do not be afraid.

19
RESURRECTION ROAD

Luke 24:1–5

But on the first day of the week, at early dawn, they came to the tomb, taking the spices that they had prepared. They found the stone rolled away from the tomb, but when they went in, they did not find the body. While they were perplexed about this, suddenly two men in dazzling clothes stood beside them. The women were terrified and bowed their faces to the ground, but the men said to them, "Why do you look for the living among the dead? He is not here but has risen.

Dear risen Savior, this resurrection thing is hard for us to understand. Too often it seems like we are trapped within our own tombs of anger, fear, distrust, or bad experiences. Help us to not be afraid anymore. Help us to see you. Amen.

"*The Lord is risen. He is risen indeed.*" In the Lutheran churches, that is the traditional Easter greeting that the Pastor offers just at the beginning of his or her Easter morning sermon.

Has anyone ever figured out The Resurrection on their own? It's Sunday morning, before dawn has broken. You are one of the women who are going to the tomb of Jesus. You are bringing certain kinds of spices, so that, at last, now that everything else is over with, Jesus' body can be properly embalmed. It's the least they could do. It turns out, that's exactly right. It was the least they could do. But at least they were doing something.

The women are on their way, and it is still dark. And, when they get there, the stone door of the tomb, high and round and heavy, has been rolled away. The body is gone. And what do the women do? Let's see. They are, according to the Bible, perplexed. They are terrified when some brightly glowing angels came. They lower their faces toward the ground. That is the least they can do. It gets better.

They go from the tomb, after some memory exercises help them to recall the words of Jesus about himself, in the right order. Suffer. Die. Resurrected. This is not easy stuff. No one was expecting this. No one. So, on the way from tomb to the sleeping disciples, they repeat, *Suffering, Dying, Resurrected*. By the time they get to the sleeping guys, they are ready. But, the men who knew Jesus best dismiss this remembrance as an "idle tale." That means that they thought the women were stark, raving, out of their minds. So much for first opinions on the resurrection. Can anyone ever understand on their own? Some of us, and I'm speaking about the men in the original encounter are still stuck in the empty tomb. That's the way it goes.

But, it isn't getting us anywhere. Jesus would like us to get somewhere with his resurrection.

I know I'm leaving Peter out of this. But, all he does is go and stick his head in the tomb. Stone. Yup. Rolled away. Tomb. Yup. Empty! And that's it. His heart is still stuck in the empty tomb. For Peter, nothing has gotten new life. Stuck in the empty tomb.

For an interesting take on what this might mean, let me tell you about my dad's office and their first computer. This was a manufacturing and shipping business, so records of what was made, what was shipped, and what we had left to sell were important. For years, most of this was recorded by hand. Then, the office in St. Louis decided that a computer would help.

It came one morning, and the rocket scientists who came with it spent the rest of the week installing and testing it. When it was ready, the new person hired for this work came into the picture. She was terribly nervous. Her job was to input every transaction of the day, with no mistakes, while being extra nice to the computer. It was a giant wheel, about 4 feet high, encased in a round, black housing, that absorbed and transmitted data. If the wheel didn't like what it was being given, it would shut down and lose all the data, even at the end of the day when it was sending information over the phone line.

Our lives were very much tied to how this inanimate wheel felt about life on any given day. This was not good. One day I walked by, looked at the wheel as it made its grinding noise and stopped.

I said, "Somebody needs to roll this stone away from the tomb."

A very nice lady employee, who was also a devout member of the Church of the Nazarene replied this way: "I wish someone would roll this thing away. Some of us are still stuck inside the tomb!"

How right she was. Perhaps the top religious question that I have in life is, "If Jesus rose from the tomb of death and sin, and then left for a new, eternal life, then how come so many of us are still stuck inside?"

At my father-in-law's funeral, over three decades ago, the fierce looking pastor started his funeral sermon with this, proclaimed in the loudest possible voice: "The Resurrection of Jesus Christ is a *fact*!" I guess sometimes that's what it takes. To get us up and awake and out of that tomb. What's the problem?

Jesus has already talked about that one. Sin. Fear. Lack of trust in God. The disciples were all over those. Experts, as it were. But, the Day of Resurrection is here, and now it's time for a new kind of action.

So, Jesus does some fantastic things. He finds Peter and forgives him. Running away? Saying you don't know me? Three times?

Forget about it. It's forgiven. Didn't you know, I'd still love you? Well, now you do. That's one thing Jesus does. And, remember, if he did it for one, he did it for everybody. Didn't you know, I'd still love you? These are the words of a freshly created world. Jesus' world. And you're in.

Jesus has a meal with his disciples. They are catching fish in the dark. They don't recognize him. He makes a breakfast of fish for them and eats it with them. They see, they begin to understand what the cross was really for. Is it hard to smile when you have a mouth full of breakfast fish? Not for them, I think. And Jesus, with a mouth similarly full of breakfast fish, says, "Didn't you know, I'd still love you? Didn't you know?"

Then, somewhere in there, Jesus finds himself walking with two broken down disciples on the way from Jerusalem (home of broken dreams) to a place called Emmaus, which is near modern Tel Aviv. It's about a good twenty-mile walk, or more. What else did these guys have to do, now?

Jesus talks with them. They refer to what happened—well, almost happened—back there in the holy city. But it didn't happen. A resurrection. It's over. Jesus spoke of the scriptures, and listened to their hearts, and just like that, they knew. It was HIM—and he WAS resurrected!

It's obviously hard work for Jesus to get these people out of the empty tomb, where the way to understand everything is by thinking about death and what dies. It's hard work, but he's doing it. Keep going, Jesus.

I was in Jerusalem once, with a bunch of pastors. We saw a lot! But if they hadn't told us to stop and look, we would have missed a 2,000-year-old Roman street, going slightly south out of the city. It went from the temple and the garden to where they threw Jesus in prison on that first Thursday night. We could see how rough that was, for anybody. For Jesus. What we were seeing was beginning to become personal.

We were invited to sit on the ancient Roman pavers, the Roman Road, and spend some time in thought. Maybe prayer. Maybe just listening to the wind and smelling the air, the city, the present and the past. So, we did. Several of the pastors began weeping softly.

I ran my hand over one of the rough stones. Then I pulled my hand away.

I thought about a couple of people I knew. I thought about my grandparents, and how, after farming their way through the Great Depression—just barely—grandpa died, leaving my grandmother with nothing. After the garage sale from hell, she moved into an apartment near us. Then, no matter where we moved, Wichita, New York, Washington D.C. (her personal favorite) and back to Illinois, she moved with us. She had, I think, the best times of her life after being beckoned out of that empty tomb. After her world fell apart, Jesus said, "Didn't you know, I'd still love you? Didn't you?"

She was just like one of the women at the empty tomb. Luke's gospel doesn't name them all. Of course not. The list is too long. Girl or guy, man or woman, you too are on that list of people at the empty tomb. You've seen the resurrection, but because of the way life works, it is possible to look at what is there, and what is not, and say "What has really happened? How does this help me now?"

And Jesus, living and new and eternal, stops by the Jerusalem Road to say hello. The hard stones are there, and the hard journey, and the hard-won history, and the victory over sin and death that still spreads and heads down that road today. But now, Jesus stops to touch a stone, your stone, and to touch you. He says, "Didn't you know, I'd still love you?"

The Lord is risen.

He is risen indeed.

20
The World's Worst Tree

Luke 13:6–9

Then he told this parable: "A man had a fig tree planted in his vineyard; and he came looking for fruit on it and found none. So, he said to the gardener, "See here! For three years I have come looking for fruit on this fig tree, and still I find none. Cut it down! Why should it be wasting the soil?' He replied, "Sir, let it alone for one more year, until I dig around it and put manure on it. If it bears fruit next year, well and good; but if not, you can cut it down."

Lord God, there is a kind of person who is always thinking that they suffer because they made God angry. And, there's a kind of person who is always seeing other's sufferings as God's punishment. Jesus cuts through the confusion about God and suffering. There's still some time to repent of sins, and that's all God wants, not the suffering. Thank you, Jesus, for making that as simple as it should be. In Your holy name we pray. Amen.

The first house my wife and I bought was in a suburb of Dallas, Texas. It had the tiniest back yard we had ever seen. And, this backyard was taken up chiefly by the worst tree in the world. It was a fruit tree of some kind. When watered, it would produce a few leaves, but that's all. It looked like a bony hand, clawing its way out of the barren earth. It had to go.

I dug it up and bought a new tree. I planted it, fertilized it, watered it, and waited. In its second year, it produced leaves, flowers, and then tiny examples of the fruit it was advertised to yield. We were happy with our backyard, now that the worst tree in the world had been replaced by this new and better specimen.

One day a major storm roared through Dallas. Shingles came off of roofs. Branches fell on power lines. My son and his best friend, responsible young men, were at our house. They called me to say that the backyard tree had fallen over onto the house. This did not seem fair. Then, back at the plant store, I was given some secret information. The trees where we lived were all doomed because the subdivision was built where cottonwood trees were. Some kind of white, fuzzy fungus infected all the trees and, when weakened, they fell over.

Then, in its place, I put in a small patio. I did not like living in a part of the world where every tree was potentially the worst tree in the world. It just wasn't worth the risk, or the heartache, or the potential for damage.

The people around Jesus didn't like living in a world where sin was the explanation for suffering. Except that they couldn't seem to help thinking and believing that way.

Their examples are not trees. The examples they give are Galileans who got themselves killed by Pontius Pilate during a riot at some religious festival. Was that God, punishing sinners? What about it, Jesus?

Another example they want to talk about concerns a big tower in a place called Siloam that fell over on eighteen perfectly nice people and crushed them to death. Or were they so nice? Maybe their sin caused it.

Jesus takes those two examples and asks the people, "Is that what you think? That God uses human pain and suffering as punishment for sin? The way Jesus talks about it, the answer would be "no." Then Jesus says something like, "If you want to talk about suffering and dying, let's talk. Unless you repent of your sins, that's your fate, your end, your destination."

It could be said that Jesus makes it easy here. I wonder if anyone has said that before? Usual human thinking sounds more like what we call *cause and effect*. You can't just repent and be forgiven, like Jesus says. Not only, we think, does sin cause suffering, we also start thinking that the suffering people have is deserved. And, saddest of all, we begin to believe that our suffering is caused and deserved. This is *cause and effect thinking*.

Cause and effect thinking is everywhere. No wonder we use it to think about God and suffering. When my sister and I were children, our parents took us to New York City. Every tourist attraction was on our list, with one notable twist. My dad had gotten us tickets to a game show, televised from Rockefeller Center.

We arrived late, but they let us in. The auditorium, arranged theatre style, was packed. The stage was lit with blinding light, highlighting everything for broadcast. The show was called "Beat the Clock." For those of you who like to be in the know, it ran from 1950 to 1961. The host was Bud Collyer, and one of the early gag writers was playwright Neil Simon.

Speaking of the gags, they were things like stacking four plates, but not using your hands. Or, chasing a balloon while carrying a cardboard box, or something. If you performed the stunt or gag before the clock ran out (55 seconds if you please) you get cash prizes in increments of $100. Even then it seemed pointless (except for the money, of course), but I mention it because it seems like a good example of cause and effect. You do something and if it's good enough, you win. Or, you do something and if it's not good enough, you get punished. That's life. Rewards for good actions, punishments for bad actions. Even with God. Life is a game show, except without the laughs.

That's why the disciples asked Jesus questions like, "This blind man here; did he sin or did his parents sin to deserve him going blind?" Jesus told them, in the gospel of John, that the one and only reason the man is blind is to receive God's mercy and show the results of God's love. Suffering, bad luck, setbacks, and losing are all for just one reason and one only. So, God can help, heal, restore, and forgive. That's it. Nothing else.

Cause and effect thinking seems natural. Even scientific. Action and opposite reaction, and that sort of thing. Maybe that's why we find ourselves reacting to things, including hardship, including suffering, including God, instead of reaching out. Like God does.

In order to get us off of cause-and-effect thinking about God and suffering, life and living, Jesus makes it simple. He says, repent. Turn away from the things that you well know are sin (including blaming people when they suffer). Repenting is turning away from sin and toward God. Ah, but what are you going to get when you are done turning and repenting? An angry, cause-and-effect God? Most of us would like to make sure before we start.

Again, Jesus makes it simple. He says you're going to turn toward a God of love, but don't wait forever. You wouldn't believe how patient God is but even that has its limits. Make it easy. Repent sooner, not later.

One rainy day a man appeared at my church office. He said that years ago he came to the church and got $100 for a car repair. He said that his car was broken, but he had lied and spent the money on drugs. Now, he had turned from those things (repent, right?) and wanted to give the money back, with interest. And he did. That day, in our very own church office, we learned about repentance, patience, and making things easy by just admitting you were wrong and saying you are sorry. The church didn't need the money, particularly, but both the guy and the pastor (me) needed another long look at a God of grace and mercy.

Jesus concludes all this with his own story about the worst tree in the world. This tree is a fruit bearing one, except that it isn't doing its job. No fruit, for three years. In Israel, then and now, soil is rocky and every fertile inch of ground counts. That's why they want to chop down the tree and give another tree a chance. But, even with the worst tree in the world, Jesus asks for another chance. Fertilize, water, and be patient. Give it another year. It may bear fruit, and it can stay.

Maybe I was wrong about the worst tree in the world being in my very own backyard. Maybe Jesus is right about repentance and forgiveness making it possible to be the best tree in the world. There are a lot of trees out there, and a lot of people who would like to know about this Jesus and forgiveness.

21

WHEN OUR FAMILY GOES FISHING

John 21:1–6

After these things Jesus showed himself again to the disciples by the Sea of Tiberias; and he showed himself in this way. Gathered there together were Simon Peter, Thomas called the Twin, Nathanael of Cana in Galilee, the sons of Zebedee, and two others of his disciples. Simon Peter said to them, "I am going fishing." They said to him, "We will go with you." They went out and got into the boat, but that night they caught nothing. Just after daybreak, Jesus stood on the beach; but the disciples did not know that it was Jesus. Jesus said to them, "Children, you have no fish, have you?" They answered him, "No." He said to them, "Cast the net to the right side of the boat, and you will find some."

Father in Heaven, perhaps John's gospel is most like our lives. After Jesus rises, his appearances don't make sense at first—well, they don't! We have trouble understanding them, but we try. And we try again. So, our prayer is simple. Help us try, and try again, when it comes to you and what you want. In Jesus' name we pray. Amen.

We went fishing as a family once. It was Memorial Day, so we were all free to be together with nature, and the lake, and the fish. Our friend offered his dock, and his little fishing boat, and a helpful hint about where to buy live bait. And, off we went. We stopped for lunch and bait and proceeded to the lake with hundreds of little fish swimming around in a plastic container.

The lake was Louisiana's largest man-made lake. My wife and my son were prepared to be dedicated fishermen. Trolling around, finding a spot, being very quiet, casting and waiting, casting and waiting. And waiting and waiting. Dedicated religiously to multitasking, I was bored out of my skull. Why don't people just phone ahead, make an appointment with the fish, catch what they need, and go home? I guess that's not the way it works.

My daughter, on that day when we went fishing together as a family, was also bored out of her skull. But she didn't know the rules of fishing, which can be summarized in one word, over and over again. Wait.

She said, "Gee, I wish I had something to do." This broke the requisite fishing silence like one of those old documentary films of an atomic bomb spreading over the landscape. "Gee, I sure wish I had something to do. I know! I'll name these fish." She was referring to the bait, of course, still merrily swimming around in their little plastic universe. "Here. This one's Molly. This one's Sarah. This one's David. There goes Melinda." Melinda?

On the day that my family went fishing, I learned how to suppress a smile. My daughter and I were as alike as my wife and son were. Dedicated fisherwomen and men on one side of the boat. Dedicated and mightily bored multitaskers on the other side. I was with my daughter one hundred percent, as she added, in her outside voice, "I wish I'd brought a book!"

My wife, the most temperate and forgiving of people, exploded. "Quiet! We're trying to catch some fish out here!" Thus, we discovered, somewhat painfully, that when a family goes fishing, you get all kinds of people in the boat. We never did catch a fish that day. And, I wonder what happened to Melinda?

Jesus' family went fishing once. Well, they went plenty of times, but this time was different. It's at the end of the gospel of John. They try and try, but they don't catch a thing. I'm guessing that their minds are on something else. Like spending three whole years with Jesus and catching nothing more than a cross, an empty tomb, and whatever it was that happened to Jesus. No wonder their fishing nets were empty.

Jesus tells them to try, try again. This turns out to be very good advice, and a very likely subject for a religious devotional about Jesus telling you and me to press on when it comes to catching fish, bringing people to church, and so forth. One day, one of us will have to write that devotional. But, today is about Jesus' family going fishing together, and all the weird things that happen when they do.

Weird, that John's gospel never directly mentions Holy Communion, or people communing together, although the disciples need it badly. Weird, also, that when John thinks about communion, he has Jesus, resurrected and ready, making a fish breakfast for disciples. Communion with fish, not bread, nor wine. Weird.

But, let me tell you about weird. It is an old English word that means the Word, as in capital "W". Like Word of God. Like living truth that comes in words to us. Weird things can be the Word of God. So, listen for them. Fish for communion is a weird word of God.

I tell my students in my World Religions class, the tendency when we talk about religion is to use lots of exalted, highfalutin' words to describe things that never get described. John avoids this. Breakfast communion with fish is weird, and it's also just so *real*. Nobody would have done this but Jesus. Nobody **could** have done this but Jesus. How real do you want your communion to be? Try letting Jesus set the menu. You'll be surprised at how real it gets.

Next weird thing. Around a charcoal campfire, Jesus and Peter talk. Everyone else seems to disappear. This is private, and intense. Remember? I bet Peter remembered it for a long time. The last time he was around a charcoal campfire, he denied his Jesus three times. Three. So, when Jesus is resurrected, and after fish communion on the beach, Jesus and Peter get real. Jesus, campfire, Peter. Light is beginning to dawn here. Jesus asks Peter three times, "Do you love me?"

Do you like technicalities? The way Jesus asks Peter this question differs each of the three times he asks it, in order to take in all aspects of a disciple's love for Jesus our Lord. And Peter's answers get a little more "huffy" each time. Then, Jesus drops his bomb. "Peter, if you love me, feed my sheep."

No technicalities here. Just the weird Word, zeroing in on the truth of the matter. Peter denies three times. Jesus asks Peter to reverse his decision three times. "I don't know Jesus at all," becomes "Yes, Lord, I love you." Jesus seems to try, try, and try again with Peter, and with us.

Once, my church family went fishing together. That is, a group of Lutheran pastors in Texas had signed up for a growth seminar for—get this—Lutheran churches that were slow growing or not growing. The joke was that *every* Lutheran church should have been there. Very funny.

Bigwigs from near and far were on hand with helpful tips about church growth. One afternoon, someone from the national church held a communion service and then told us to go fish, cast our nets and see what happens.

That meant going out two by two in the neighborhood around the church where we were meeting, knocking on doors, and inviting people to church. It was one of the most interesting days of my life.

Some people were not home. Like me, you might have been a little relieved. Some people were at home, and wanted to witness to me about their zippy, Spirit-filled, activity inflated churches. I listened carefully. Joy in church membership is always to be duly noted and appreciated. Like me, you might have been glad.

Then, as the sun was going down, the last house on the block presented the last door for knocking. A man came out. About 40 years old. Casually dressed. A scowl on his face. I'm not going to any church he said (I had guessed!), but maybe you'll have something to say about my problem. My wife died of cancer six months ago. It hurt like nothing else, ever. And God? Where is God? That's what I'd like to know. Maybe you can answer.

I froze, there on the front porch of the last house with the last door for knocking on, and the last thing I thought I'd hear that day. Like me, you might have been thinking about a way out of this. Too much pain. Too few answers. I don't even really like answers when people are hurting with that kind of depth and brokenness. So, I decided to stay and listen as long as our conversation would support my presence there on this guy's porch.

He shook my hand when I left. He said, "thanks."

He was not in church on Sunday.

As far as I could tell, the only thing that happened that day was that God gave him practice opening his door to someone, to something. And, as Jesus has it, God keeps visiting the charcoal campfires of death and defeat, and asking life-giving questions, once, twice, thrice, and more. Like me, you might have been excited to be a part of this resurrection Jesus, and what he means by fishing. Then, a door will open, and God once more begins his work of try, try, try again. Like me, you might be praying that it's you, right there, when that door opens.

22

TAKE MY HEART, BUT PLEASE DON'T BREAK IT

John 13:34–35

> *I give you a new commandment, that you love one another. Just as I have loved you, you also should love one another. By this everyone will know that you are my disciples, if you have love for one another.*

Father, Jesus teaches love. Father, Jesus calls his betrayal his glory. Is love that automatic with him, that strong? Whenever we think about Jesus and his kind of love, something comes along to try and ruin it. Thank you for showing us that Jesus rises above that kind of disappointment. Do you think we could, too? In Christ's name we pray. Amen.

Vacation time. My wife and I found a weekend sitter for dogs and kids, and we were off! Off to the glories of small town America and a bed and breakfast. It was great. The house we stayed in was an imposing Queen Anne style, with a wraparound porch and a turret with a spire. The first night, the owner told us the story of the house. Light a candle, lock the door, and pull up your chair. This is the story of the house.

Well, it's not that scary, really. But it is unusual. The house was built over 100 years ago. A husband and wife had it constructed for the family they wanted to raise. They added touches of their own. One was a removable top of the base of the grand staircase. They stored the house deed there, so that if there were a fire, you could grab it on the way out the door. There was also a huge copper tub in the attic, with pipes that carried water to sinks and bathtubs. That tub had been sold for scrap in the 1960's, but the idea was still there. This was a super deluxe house, in its day. And, in a way, it still was.

The husband and wife died of old age, leaving behind a grown daughter. The daughter was, ah, socially awkward, one might say. And one did say, because everyone else said so, too, and sometimes the words they used were cruel. People laughed at her behind her back.

If she came to your house for tea, or a shower, or some other reason, one would have to count the silver. She had a habit of stealing forks and spoons and knives and tiny pickle forks, whatnot.

After the war, people changed. And the daughter only got worse. She was no longer invited out. Children would throw an occasional rock at the house, but nothing else happened for a long time. A new, modern house was built next door in the 1950's.

By then, the daughter had become a recluse. She shut off the rooms upstairs, including the turret room with the curved-glass windows and the wonderful view. She slept in the kitchen, on a cot. There she could keep warm.

During the daughter's decline, a family moved into the 1950's house next door. The new family had a daughter, too. The new daughter, a teenager, developed a curiosity about the house next door, with rumors of a lady kleptomaniac who slept in the kitchen.

The new daughter went up the porch steps and twisted the little thumbscrew on the old, rusty doorbell. It rang. The new daughter's heart stopped for a second. After some waiting, and some shuffling noises inside, the door opened. This was the beginning of summer.

Many daily visits began to turn the tide. The old daughter and the new one next door began to trust each other. They sat in the crumbling living room and talked for hours at each visit. The new daughter asked to see the rest of the house. "In time," the old woman said.

When it finally happened, that tour, the new daughter felt herself falling in love with a neglected, dusty house, once grand and with the house's owner, who was also kind of neglected, dusty, and very lonely.

The new daughter graduated from high school. The girl went to college. She graduated and took a job in Chicago, on Michigan Avenue, as the manager of a company that sold fur coats to the carriage trade. The old daughter died peacefully in her house on the cot in the kitchen, surrounded by the silver that she once took, and perhaps remembering the hand of love and friendship she once was given.

Jesus chooses funny places to teach us about loving, doesn't he? One place was the Upper Room, right after Judas quickly, quietly leaves the others to betray Jesus and make him die. Maybe I wouldn't be thinking about love. But Jesus does. He gathers the remaining disciples in close. He says, "I give you a new commandment, that you love one another. Just as I have loved you, you also should love one another." John always has Jesus repeat important teachings a few times, so that they sink in and sound as truthful as they are. As powerful as they can be. But this time, I think you can just about hear Jesus doing the repeating for real. Love. Love one another. Like I loved you, now you do it. Love.

All brass and sass is the old Nat King Cole song, *Love is made for me and you*. Lyrics, please.

> *L is for the way you look at me*
> *O is for the only one I see*
> *V is very, very extraordinary*
> *E is even more than anyone that you adore can*
> *Love is all that I can give to you*
> *Love is more than just a game for two*
> *Two in love can make it*
> *Take my heart and please don't break it*
> *Love was made for me and you*

How about that? Not only does Nat King Cole spell it out for you, L-O-V-E, but there's a little prayer being prayed inside of all that brass and sass. "Take my heart, and please don't break it."

Sometimes I quote songs like this, in a kind of unexpected way (sometimes I even sing them) to change things up a little bit. The last thing I want when I come to church is someone telling me, "*Alright you Christians. Start loving* **now**! *Jesus says so! Love everybody. Don't leave out even one! Even rotten people who steal your silver … or open fire in shopping malls or wish to work evil in the world."* I don't like that approach because I think that ordering people to love others is just useless.

"*OK, Christians. On your mark, get set, love!*" See what I mean?

It's worth noting that when Jesus tells us to love (the great commandment, and beyond), it's after he spends a third of John's gospel (and OK, a third of his ministry) telling people that the only path for Jesus is suffering and death and resurrection. Then, after Jesus tells us to love one another, he spends the last third of John's gospel finding his way to the cross and dying there and rising too.

We answer with a prayer. "*OK, Jesus. Take my heart, but please don't break it. I know that if I reach out, if I extend myself, it would be rough. Maybe risky. Maybe nothing would happen. Maybe people would throw rocks at my door, or laugh at me, or break my heart. Jesus, you may be asking too much. Take my heart, but please don't break it.*"

But alas! Everything costs something, doesn't it? And it's true that the price to pay for having a church family, or a family of any kind, or much of anything worthwhile, is the cost of a broken heart. People can be cruel. But, do you really want that to be the last thing you say about your life with Christ and other Christians?

Oh, sorry. I beg your pardon! Here I am, after what I said, giving you marching orders about love. Why don't I just finish the story of the daughters, old and new?

One day there was a frightful commotion at the old daughter's house. Her funeral was over—no one went. Now they were going through the house, room by room, getting her things ready for auction. The new daughter's mom, from her 1950's house next door, called her daughter in Chicago. She was in the middle of selling a fur coat. She finished the coat sale, then arranged for financing for what she was about to do.

The last thing they auctioned off was the house itself. It was not in great shape, which meant that the bids were low. The new daughter bid by phone from the fur store. She won. She was so excited that she jumped up and down, so that fur-clad matrons looked her up and down. What an eccentric! New daughter, old daughter. Maybe love makes you that way.

The day the daughter got the key to the old mansion; her plans were well in place. She had always wanted to create a warm and welcoming place for tired travelers. A place where they could relax, be fed, renew. It was a gift that she was given once when she was new in the little town on the dusty prairie where her parents had just moved. Her gift was from a misunderstood, lonely, and slightly off-kilter old lady who invited her in. The rattling behind her door might have been some pilfered silver, or her broken heart. It didn't matter anymore. Love opened a door.

Now, the new daughter would open that same door many times, magnifying the friendship that she had once before, and sharing a thing we would call love.

Jesus has a strange way of talking about loving each other at strange moments. Like when we are not in a loving mood. Like when we are locked away with a broken heart. Like when we stand on a porch, or an opportunity, with a lump in the throat. A strange way of talking about love at strange times.

He says, *"I give you a new commandment, that you love one another. By this everyone will know that you are my disciples, if you have love for one another."*

23
GRAND CANYON CALLING

John 10:27–28

My sheep hear my voice. I know them, and they follow me. I give them eternal life, and they will never perish. No one will snatch them out of my hand.

Father, sometimes we have the creeping suspicion that hearing Jesus' voice and following him is mostly talk and something we can't do too well. Yes, I know, there are a few to whom it comes naturally, but not me. Be with me when I doubt I can hear your voice and be with me when I hear something, (perhaps a whisper) and be with me when I try to follow. Accept my doubt and rekindle my faith. In Christ's name I pray. Amen.

A Buick LeSabre is no match for the steep and ascending highway out of the Arizona valley, and up to the Grand Canyon. My wife and I had been there before and wanted to see it again. Something happened inside of me the first time I was there. The National Park Service guide talked about tourists 100 years ago, driving back and forth across the north rim, now closed, in their Model T's.

The romance of the past!

Also, there were no guard rails around the southern rim. Except for common sense, which said that if you didn't want to fall over the side, you stayed away from the edge. I like that it reminds me of my feelings about God. Stay a little back from the rim, for safety's sake. Maybe you know what I mean. Or, perhaps not.

Our daughter, who thought the Grand Canyon would be just another roadside attraction, was not happy with us, our Buick, or our choice of destination. That is, until we arrived. Then, the vastness of the place took our collective breath away.

While we're there in this story, maybe I can work in a few quick analogies between the largest known hole in the world and our faith. I'd like to try.

Since our previous visit, the National Park Service had placed plenty of solid guardrails around the south rim, where the tourists were. A wonderful experience was now guaranteed, without tourists having to judge just how far they could go.

The Park Service was also thinking about building that glass and steel catwalk, cantilevered out and over the canyon, so that one could experience what it was like to give oneself over to the vastness of the place, without doing so in reality.

I was not willing, nor am I now, to go even that far, when it comes to canyons, or following God. No. Not me. I like the dreamy feeling that comes from eating in the Harvey dining room there at the Canyon, where tourists tied up their Model T Fords a century ago and dined. I like my religion kind of dreamy, with good experiences that are safe for me.

With our heads buzzing slightly from the work of analogies, let's see what Jesus is doing in the gospel of John. He's in the Jerusalem temple. It is winter, and Hanukkah is going on, with the menorah, the festivals, and thinking about God's past and miraculous deeds for his people. Sounds good, huh? Not for Jesus. He's strolling through Solomon's Portico, the temple porch where judges used to examine the credentials of religious leaders to see what they were up to and if they measured up. Although there were no judges in residence, Jesus was there because he knew he was being judged.

In fact, see what happens next. Jesus' detractors come up upon him. "*How do we know?*" they say. "*If you are really the Messiah, then tell us.*"

Proof is reassuring. It's hard to be mad at these detractors who put grey clouds over Jesus' Hanukkah celebration. You see, I'm sometimes a doubter, too.

Jesus knows what to say. He says it for the people he loves, who carry doubt and faith around like two suitcases. He says it for the people who are going to "get it" about him, either today or some future point. He says, "*Those who know my voice follow me.*"

Jesus knows what to say. Hear Jesus and his voice. And follow. No tame religious experiences for the ones who hear and follow. A call to action. And then: action. Lots of people talk about baptism being that call to action. It is. And for many of us, it's enough. Baptismal water running low? Bread and wine are here for the journey. Following Jesus builds up a spiritual hunger as big as the Grand Canyon, and only Jesus can fill it. Eat. Drink. It is for you.

This is why I don't always "freak out" or cower in fear or doubt completely when Jesus opens up various Grand Canyon-like pits of need and suffering in front of me, although I occasionally do. That's when guardrails and glass walkways are no good at all. Forgiveness is needed, and it comes.

But, we were on our way to the next Grand Canyon. This time, it was an elderly lady, living in her daughter's home, frail with Osteoporosis and advanced age. The daughter was overburdened with her care. She would ask me to sit with her mom and talk while she picked up some groceries, or just went for a walk somewhere. I was glad to assist. I was thinking that I had filled another void in another life. Good for me!

But, not so fast. One time when I came to call, the mom was in her room, not able to get out of her bed. Speechless, she held up her arm, which was covered in bruises, and some blood. She showed me her arm, and looked into my eyes, pleading. What do you think I was being asked to see?

This was one of those times when I carefully backed away from the edge of a bad situation. I still came back, still gave communion, and still sat for long talks while the daughter went out into the sunshine and relieved some caregiver fatigue.

Now, later, I wish that I had listened to Jesus' soft but persistent voice when I looked at the mother's damaged arm and into her pleading eyes. Elder abuse.

I wish I had listened more carefully. I'm sure the mom did, too.

OK—I did listen in a way. I did follow up to a point. I stayed in the situation, prayed in the situation, did what I could. I don't think we even knew about elder abuse in those days. But, no. I'm not going to say that. Excuses are for the birds. People who follow and serve do come up with doubts. Doubts about what they do, what they leave undone, and what God may have in mind for them. I know that's true.

When doubts and faith go together, the only thing that works when things don't work out is … forgiveness. For the daughter. For me.

I think that we, as the church, do a good job of asking people to respond to God's call—or calls, we should say, because there are plenty of them, all the time, for all of us. Calls to service and love and sacrifice. The vehicles by which we receive the calls are baptism, reading the Bible, or simply hearing what Jesus is saying to us. Churches do a pretty good job of reminding people to keep listening for those calls.

Today, I'd like to follow up on that. Operator please. I'd like to be connected to Jesus. I'd like to be connected to Jesus when I hear his call but do an imperfect job. That's rough on me and the people who rely on me. I'd like to be connected to Jesus when I find that the going is a little more than I can manage gracefully.

I'd like to be connected to Jesus when I see the immensity of need, like a canyon that a person might fall into and never be heard from again. I'd like a connection with Jesus when doubt and faith are in harmony with one another, but I'm not in harmony with anything at all.

When I am at the place of baptism, Jesus, you are there with your call for me to serve. When I am at your table, Jesus, you are there with food and comfort for my faith, and my doubts. When I read your Word and understand what you ask of us when we follow, I see the words of forgiveness and life on the page, and they *spring* to life. They are for me.

Am I just another cold breeze on the temple porch for you, Jesus? Or am I one who hears your voice, knows your Messiahship, and who follows you? I would like to be connected to you. So, you simply say, "*Put the call through. I am here for you, in cross and resurrection. I am here.*"

How simple your Messiahship is, Jesus. How simple. How powerful. Speak to us again. Call us.

24

WHEN *YOU* DECIDE

Luke 10:38–39

> *Now as they went on their way, he entered a certain village,*
> *where a woman named Martha welcomed him into her*
> *home. She had a sister named Mary, who sat at the Lord's*
> *feet and listened to what he was saying.*

Once again, Jesus, you have come to visit Mary and Martha. Just
between you and me, the scene between the living room and the kitchen
seems kind of tense. Churches are tense. Families are tense, sometimes.
But you are there. And because you are, we can make some choices about
what kind of Christian we want to be and that will shape what goes on
between the living room and the kitchen. Thank you, Jesus. AMEN.

Once again the college students in the little class that I teach
have given me something to think about. They come from
working class backgrounds, and usually have a very practical
way of looking at life that has its roots in family, in church, and in
the value of hard work. In other words, they are like almost everyone
else, except that they spend their evenings trying to get a degree.

The class in question here is Religion 134, Western Religions. We look at a list of religions, including Wicca, Rastafarianism, Druidism, and Voodoo. It turns out that when Ricky Ricardo was singing "Babaloo!" on *I Love Lucy,* he was borrowing a word from Voodoo. Heavens! Religion is full of surprises.

The three big religions we study are Islam, Judaism, and Christianity. The last assignment for the last class is to select a religion and several issues that confront it. The learning team will discuss those issues, citing five sources. Then they will compare the same issues with what's going on in the other two religions. It all comes back into the classroom in a thirty-minute Power Point presentation. Guess who's learning the most about religion in modern life at this point? That's right. That would be me.

Christianity, I'm learning, is in a state of change. I ask the class point-blank how they see the future of the faith; where it's going.

Here are the answers.

> 1) No more overpaid clergy. In fact, maybe *no* trained clergy.
> 2) No more big-box churches. In fact, maybe no church buildings at all. Or, maybe the smaller churches are on their way out, with several big churches taking over.
> 3) Worship could be in people's homes, with strict following of the rules in the Bible. During worship there could be simple hymns and sharing of stories about faith struggles. Then, a meal.

If you ask a question, you'd better be prepared to hear the answer, right? So, there I am, in my suit and tie, standing at the head of the class, with everyone knowing that I'm a pastor. I am fighting with myself about a response to no church buildings, no pastors. Should I remind the class that I am a trained clergyman, who has forgotten more Greek, Latin, and Hebrew than they will ever learn? Or, should I tell them that I've forgotten practically all of it, and that I am a Christian, curious about the future, just as they are?

I decide to keep my mouth shut. Remember? If you ask a question, you'd better be prepared to hear the answer.

Besides, silence sometimes forces thought, and that's what's happening to me. I'm thinking that if they are right, church would look a lot like the gospel today, with Jesus at Mary and Martha's house, kicking back, waiting for what smells like a fantastic dinner.

Utopia, right? Take away all the silly trappings of church, get back to the essence of things, and your problems disappear. Right?

Or, not.

Mary and Martha are having a fight. Well, no they're not. Martha is doing all the fighting. She's not just making one of her usual fantastic dinners, she's making life hell for both Mary and Jesus. She's trying to drag Jesus into her fight. "Jesus, make Mary help me in the kitchen."

By the way, here comes my not-so-patented advice about how to read the Bible. Always look for the part in the story where things get unusual. There you will see God at work.

The unusual plot twist here is that Mary is sitting at Jesus' feet like a student. Men and men only were students in those days, not women. Women showed their devotion in the kitchen, whipping up a killer meal. What we see here is vastly different than the usual, what we call cultural norms, unless we're involved in them. Then we either call them liberating (Go, Mary!) or something more negative (Yea, Martha!). Which one would you be saying?

The upshot of all this, I believe, is that you decide what your church is going to be like when you decide what *you* are going to be like.

Here is an incident from the front lines. Women's Day of Prayer used to take over the small town I pastored in for one day a year. The Methodist Pastor's wife, Marilyn, was bossy and grim. The Presbyterian Pastor's wife ought to have been named Mary. She was relaxed and gracious, an expert at smelling the roses. While the two of them stood at the top of the huge staircase in the Presbyterian Church, the Prayer service was about to begin. Marilyn was managing everything, giving orders, worrying over last minute details, making Mary's life miserable by taking over everything!

Calmly, Mary looked at Marilyn, took a breath, and said, "Marilyn, if you give me one more order, I will personally knock you down these stairs." The church community responded with interest to these words. The moment belonged to Mary, and everyone was listening. Mary continued, "Marilyn, why don't you go into the sanctuary and pray? That's why we're here." And so, that is what Marilyn did.

The point is the same. You decide what your church is going to be when you decide what *you* are going to be.

Are you innovative, or traditional? Nah! That's not the real question. Any church or family or workplace has room for both. Plenty of room. The real question is, are you a bossy manipulator, or an eager student?

While you mull that over for a minute, please also notice that I am not particularly worried about whether the church of the future will pay premium prices for well-educated clergy. I am also not worried about whether Christians will continue to erect fabulous church buildings, decorate them with precious metals and art glass, and adequately air condition them. Those things have a way of working themselves out without hurting people if you know who you are at the get-go.

I am more worried about whether, at heart, I am a bossy manipulator or a worshipper, an eager student, a Mary. I know that being a *Mary* is right, doing what it takes to learn from Jesus and worship him. By the way, you won't find a lot of formal worship in the gospels. Instead people worship Jesus by sitting at his feet (like Mary), kneeling, prostrating themselves, or washing him with expensive perfumes. Worship happens in daily life long before it happens in a church. It is ever so.

When I was growing up, I was a bossy manipulator waiting to burst upon the local church scene. Things that kept me up at night were mistakes made in worship, or at the altar, or perhaps something said that was not theologically correct. Was I a bore? What do you think— of course I was!

It turns out that this was a family trait. My mother's mother mothered with a heavy hand and a loud voice, issuing commands. After grandpa died, she lived with us for a while, being a bossy grandmother. We still loved her. But those habits rubbed off on me, I guess.

Then, much later, grandma got very sick. Being bossy only goes so far when you are in the hospital, when you lose your legs, when you have to make up your mind every day just to try.

I lived on the other side of the state, but when things got bad, my mother would call me and ask me to come right away and bring communion. So, I did.

One time, near the end of grandma's life, she surprised me. I had brought her communion. She stopped me as I was about to give her the bread and wine. She said, "Before this is over, there will be many tears and pain. But we will learn about God, and we will be blessed." Those seemed to me to be the words of a Mary, coming true and clear from an old-time Martha. It seems like your church, or your hospital room, or your home, will be what it is when you decide what *you* are.

Note to self: you are what you were **baptized** to be; a child of God, a student and worshipper and friend of Jesus, powered up each day by the Holy Spirit. You can choose to be that. It's there for you to choose. Yours, if you want it.

Note to self: the next time I teach Religion 134, Western Religions, remember that what it takes to be the church is a combination of the Word of God (which is Bible and preaching and teaching) and the Sacraments (baptism and communion).

Note to self: then, relax. And say, *Amen.*

25

LIKE BREAD AT MIDNIGHT

Luke 11:1–4

He was praying in a certain place, and after he had finished, one of his disciples said to him, "Lord, teach us to pray, as John taught his disciples." He said to them, "When you pray, say: Father, hallowed be your name. Your kingdom come. Give us each day our daily bread. And forgive us our sins, for we ourselves forgive everyone indebted to us. And do not bring us to the time of trial."

Our Father (not just mine, for we all share the same God) in Heaven, hallowed be thy name (meaning, God, show how holy your name is in your answers to us), thy kingdom come, thy will be done (saying, we'd like it done where we live, and how we live) on earth, as it is in heaven. Give us this day our daily bread (but not one bit more, so we forget you and think about the bread, or the job, or the money we need), and forgive us our trespasses as we forgive those who trespass against us (because without forgiveness, all relationships would dry up and vanish). For the kingdom, and the power, and the glory are yours, Father, (because you know how to handle it better than we do). Amen.

L ord, teach us to pray.

So, that is exactly what Jesus did.

When I was serving as a volunteer trauma chaplain, the other volunteers were pastors of independent churches. They saw prayer differently than I did.

One pastor from Africa used to pray by jumping up and singing a praise hymn. Prayer was no more or less than being thankful to God, with body, mind, and spirit. People kind of liked it. I had forgotten that Christianity is a musical.

Another pastor felt like he could ask God for all sorts of things, like a better job, a better car, new suits! He could do this asking boldly, because God had asked him to become a servant of his kingdom in the world and promised to sustain him. I must say, I had not ever dared to think of heaven as a kind of Overstock.com where you could place your order and get what you needed. Where else does everything come from, but from God?

These people were teaching me things about prayer, mostly by showing me things about prayer, that my Lutheran background did not like very much. Were they right or wrong about prayers and praying?

A little old lady in Louisiana that I used to visit had it just the other way around about prayer. She said that in catechism class, or confirmation, the pastor told them never, ever to pray for their own needs. It was too selfish. Only pray for others, and only pray, "thy will be done." Let God do the rest. Never presume that you might know what to ask God for.

Golly! How strict is that? Was her pastor right or wrong about prayers and praying?

I once did a sermon series called "The Theology of Marilyn Monroe." I showed film clips and highlighted a few points, and we talked about what the points really meant. Needless to say, this was never written up in any scholarly journals.

In one movie, *Niagara,* Marilyn is a waitress who marries a Wisconsin farmer with violent tendencies. They go to Niagara Falls to renew their shaky marriage. Meanwhile, they meet a nice young couple who are staying at the same motel.

The husband finds out Marilyn has a boyfriend and kills her in the famous Niagara Falls bell tower. Then, the husband, on the lam, takes the boat that the young couple are going to use to go fishing. The nice young woman is now on board with the murderous husband of the now dead Marilyn Monroe. The boat has no gas. They are headed for the falls. Danger ahead!

The nice young husband stands on the shore, saying "scuttle it, scuttle it." They do, knocking out the sea cocks, or boat plugs, letting the water in, so the boat will sink and won't go over the falls.

I hope you're still with me because we are getting to the theology part, and to the end of the movie. The woman in the boat is saved by jumping on a rock, the killer husband goes over the falls. In the last line of the movie, the nice young husband says, "I'll bet that's the first time anyone has used "scuttle it" as a prayer, and had it answered."

There. That's the theology of Marilyn Monroe. *Prayer is what you need to say to God, when you need to say it.*

OK, then. What about if you pray for something important, and God doesn't give it to you? That's probably why the disciples say to Jesus, "Lord, teach us to pray." That sort of asking, and not getting, happens with troubling frequency. Lord, teach us to pray.

Or, what happens if you pray for something, like a great job, or a nice spouse, and someone else gets it instead? Is God's aim at fault? The disciples wisely ask Jesus to teach them to pray.

This prayer from Jesus for our use is a good guide for what to say when praying. It's about receiving a relationship from God and maintaining it, creature (us) to creator.

It's about trusting God for daily bread, including job, food, money, house, clothing, and more. Trust is the opposite of worry and grasping. For some people, is anything ever enough? For some people, the answer is no. For certain places in all of our hearts, the answer is no as well. So, prayer changes your heart.

But what is prayer is supposed to do? Is it to get things from God, or to praise, praise, praise? Is it so unbearably modest that you can't really ask for anything? Or, is it like in the movie *Niagara,* where a prayer is simple and loving, desperate and trusting at the same moment?

Jesus did not have movies to illustrate his points about prayer, which is maybe a good thing. Instead, he had daily life! That's where most prayer occurs anyway.

We get self-conscious when praying, (O God, most high … is that the right way? Or, O holy Adonai, source of all good things … is that better sounding?) By this time, you have drifted off and are thinking of other things. No prayers are getting prayed. This happens to me all the time. And I'm the one who is supposed to know how to pray a prayer.

So, Jesus goes back to daily life. In his day, hospitality was king. I wish it still were. But life and the devil and selfishness and lack of trust are powerful things. Not more powerful than God, though. We ought to pray to him about it.

Here we go, following the rest of Luke chapter 11. Prayer is like having guests at midnight, and you forgot to go to the store. There is nothing in the kitchen except a very old yogurt and a frozen lasagna that would take too long to cook. So, because hospitality is king, you go next door and ask for three loaves of bread. Sandwiches! Why not?

The neighbor has his own priorities, like sleep! He's tucked in for the night, in the one room that everybody had in those days, for cooking, sleeping, and so on. The neighbor would have to wake everyone up to get the bread out. Jesus says, where God is concerned, it's OK to keep asking, all night if you have to, so that the neighbor gets the lead out and gives you the bread, or so that God hears you. Informally. Urgently. With some kind of response.

The word that Jesus uses here is supposed to read, *persistence,* but that's way too polite for what Jesus has in mind. Instead, the real word is *shamelessness.* That's right. What Jesus says about prayer is to be "shameless" in prayer. Take it to the Lord in prayer. All of it. Gather your prayers like roses, thorns included.

This would mean that everyone we talked about, the guy in the movie praying for his wife, the chaplain guy praying for more creature comforts, the praise, praise, praise guy, and the ladylike little old lady who was learning to pray for herself and loved ones, all of those people were right, according to Jesus. Pray shamelessly. Don't give up. Think your voice is getting a little strident? Think again. Whatever you have to say—and not just the nice stuff—is music to God's ears. Jesus commands us to pray for that very reason.

In the end of this time of teaching about prayer, Jesus describes all kinds of relationships where *asking* is happening. Kids ask their parents for an egg and get a scorpion. Or, they ask for a fish and get a snake. This is all about the disappointment and sometimes treachery of living in the world we live in. Jesus knows all about it. And he's asking that you raise your voice, the one in your heart and the one in your throat shamelessly, like the guy who wouldn't give up until he got his bread.

Why? So, we never lose the habit of talking to God, and those constant conversations that Jesus calls shameless change the voice in our hearts and the voice in our throats to sound more like his—full of grace and hope. Because we can talk to a God we can trust.

26

Welcoming

Matthew 10:40–42

> *Whoever welcomes you welcomes me, and whoever welcomes me welcomes the one who sent me. Whoever welcomes a prophet in the name of a prophet will receive a prophet's reward; and whoever welcomes a righteous person in the name of a righteous person will receive the reward of the righteous; and whoever gives even a cup of cold water to one of these little ones in the name of a disciple—truly I tell you, none of these will lose their reward.*

God, there is always something you are calling me to do. You are honest with me, and use words like prophetic and righteous, which mean if I did what you wanted it would be a bit like you doing it. I hear it as a dare. You say it as love. Help me hear love, when I respond.

Jonah was a volunteer in a big Lutheran church. Life was not all rosy there. The senior pastor was a former missionary who maintained extremely high standards for professional performance for his staff. There were no warm fuzzy emotions for being a staff person in this particular church. You either made the cut or made your way to the door.

The youth pastor was young himself, with a wife, but no children. He told Jonah once that because of the demands made on him by his ministry, he feared that he might be relying too much on his nightly Black Russian, which is a drink made with vodka and Kahlua. The youth pastor also told of nights when he did family counseling, which meant talking either husband or wife out of acting out frustrations with marriage and family and staying out of bars in local strip malls.

The youth pastor explained something to Jonah. He said that most of the people in their church had a lot of challenges. They were not high up on the socio-economic scale. In most families, both husband and wife worked, and the so-called split shift kept husband and wife on schedules that changed often and because of those schedules, almost always kept them from seeing each other. Their families were fed, but the stress took its toll. Most of the youth that he and Jonah ministered to came from families where split shifts and marital fights were pretty common. This, the youth pastor explained to the young Jonah, fresh out of college, was a community where people were either on their way up or their way down and out, and that was the ministry that was happening there, in that church, at that time and in that place.

There was a big youth confirmation retreat in the middle of winter. Jonah volunteered to go along and teach. He was so excited that he forgot his sleeping bag and pillow, so he slept on a bare cot with an old blanket someone found on one of the school busses that carried the 100 plus kids to the camp.

Jonah had never felt so alive. The kids responded to him and the classes they had together really came alive. On the first night, all the boys in Jonah's cabin decided to break out and go exploring in the winter chill when Jonah had fallen asleep. Jonah had never been faced with this before but managed to talk his way through it and talk the kids out of it.

The kids stayed warm and dry that night, and a bond between counselor Jonah and conformation kids was made.

In class one day, Jonah discovered that the kids he was teaching knew nothing of any kind of Christian relationship between men and women, also known as marriage. All the kids had to go by was what they saw on TV, which was about people exchanging money for intimacy. Jonah scrapped that afternoon's lesson plan and went through what he knew about relationships in the Bible. Jonah found to his surprise that he wasn't preachy or legalistic because he didn't feel that way about relationships. He had the kids in the palm of his hand, and they felt that God was promising them a better way. This was exhilarating to Jonah. He had never felt such power. He began to wonder if he should find a way to make it continue, to perhaps become a youth pastor. Or something. Maybe. And he prayed about it. The kids really seemed to like him, and so did the youth pastor and the other counselors. What, God, is going on here? That was Jonah's prayer.

The northern snows melted, the trees leafed out, and summer came. When it did, Jonah prepared to search for a summer job to help with his school expenses.

At that point, he had a final meeting with the youth pastor who surprised Jonah by offering him a full-time position as youth director. What do you think Jonah did?

Before we know what happened, it's time to talk about the short, but important little gospel reading for today.

Here's what is going on. Jesus has asked the disciples to go out into the world. He tells them, in a passage that is as famous as it is misunderstood, that they must go out into the lanes and byways of the land without extra clothes, money, or sandals. In short, they must do God's work by relying on the welcoming nature of the communities they visit.

Oh, yes! This is the part where Jesus tells them to shake the dust off their sandals if people don't receive them kindly. This is true, but the main thing is that the disciples make themselves totally available to the people they work with, eat with, stay with. The disciples are, as it were, at the mercy of the communities they are in. I wonder if Jonah felt that way about getting deeper into youth work? It does raise some questions, doesn't it?

To move on, Jesus then tells these disciples about what is to come. The predictions are not encouraging. The word "cross" is mentioned several times. Uh oh. You know what that means. Everybody does. And it's not good.

Then, Jesus offers this teaching. We hear about it again in this gospel reading. "Expect," Jesus says, "a prophet's welcome for a prophet's work." That probably means that prophets carry messages from God to the people. Those messages are usually about shaping up, sharpening up focus, and getting back to trust in God instead of various other things. These are hard messages.

Jonah the youth worker had a bit of this kind of experience when he dropped his lesson plan and taught his kids about what a Christian relationship involving intimacy could mean, and what it should not mean. Jonah was lucky. His audience was receptive and hungry for what he had to say. It doesn't always work that way. Jonah found that out when he got back to the city.

The same confirmation kids who had been so receptive in that retreat environment, when they returned to their day-to-day lives, would tear apart their down jackets and blow the feather stuffing at him when he turned to write on the board. What had happened? How did the relationship with those kids change once they were back home? A prophet's welcome is seldom warm. Is Jesus promising something here or giving a warning? That was one of the things Jonah was trying hard to figure out.

Also, Jesus talks about a community welcoming a righteous person. In the Bible, righteousness is the same word as justice. *Self-righteousness* is always wanting justice for yourself. *True righteousness* is wanting justice for other people and doing your best to get it. In other words, justice means giving people who are down and out the kind of treatment here and now that you would want if you were down and out. That sounds difficult, too. At least it does to me.

I have the feeling that our friend Jonah was wondering about that, too. Church life can be tough, especially when you put your heart into it. Teaching the Bible to people's needs? Counseling an unfaithful spouse in a local bar? Working under an unyielding and somewhat perfectionistic supervising pastor? What kind of righteous reward was that going to bring?

Jonah began to weigh the possibilities. He had a nice job in an air-conditioned office waiting for him at home. His steady girlfriend would be working in the same office. They could have a great summer together. It would be fun, and not too demanding. Or, he could take the youth pastor's dare and become the youth director. Jonah didn't think that the words "prophetic" or "righteous" had anything to do with his qualifications, if indeed he had any at all. But, God tends to define these things for us while we are trying to live them out. You just never know with God, do you? That's what Jonah was saying about it.

But, back to Jesus. The third thing Jesus talked about, after being prophetic and being righteous, was giving a cold cup of water to someone he called "one of these little ones." Could he have meant children? Could he have meant the kids in Jonah's youth group? Could Jesus have meant anybody who felt little in the wide, big world we all know, who needed some encouragement?

Jonah thought and thought. He even remembered to pray. That Jesus, he does this sort of thing all the time! He uses words like justice and righteousness, which stir the heart and promise a better world—and promises ordinary people a share in helping to make it that way! It really does stir the heart. Or, is that what they call the Holy Spirit?

Jonah said, "I don't know!" He was truly confused. Because he knew that any service to God would be hard, if he bothered to pursue it further, understanding that God was gently daring him to take it on. Jonah felt alternately awed by this God and a bit resentful.

I know what Jonah did. I know because _I am_ Jonah. Jonah went home that summer, worked in a nice, air-conditioned office with his girlfriend, whom he later married. He said no to the youth pastor and did not become the youth director. Jonah—well, me—was relieved that he could get away from the call to be prophetic and righteous for a little while longer, maybe until after seminary and he was ordained. The cup of cold water would have to stay on the shelf for a while, where it would go lukewarm and evaporate. Oh, well.

Sometimes Jonah—well, that would be me—feels like he has gotten too good at delaying the life that Jesus is talking about, with words to describe it like justice, or righteousness, and being prophetic, and actions basic and true, like giving that cold cup of water to one who feels little in this big world. Delays are allowable. Other opportunities will come along.

Meanwhile, Jesus is waiting. Or, like the old hymn says, Jesus is calling. Jonah wondered why Jesus' voice never got tired or scratchy or wears out from the calling. Jonah finally realized that behind the youth pastor's dare to join him in his work, there was a Jesus who called him simply because he loved Jonah, and it filled Jesus' heart to have one that he loved as much as Jonah working alongside him. That's all it was ever about. And Jonah—that would be me—has been doing just that for nearly forty years.

27

THE "I'M EARLY" LADY

Romans 7:15–18

> *I do not understand my own actions. For I do not do what I want, but I do the very thing I hate. Now if I do what I do not want, I agree that the law is good. But in fact, it is no longer I that do it, but sin that dwells within me. For I know that nothing good dwells within me, that is, in my flesh. I can will what is right, but I cannot do it.*

St. Paul has some good things to say to us, God. These things were powerful in the first century. But, how about now? Paul says that a part of us is sinful and can't help it. But, then, the part of us that is you is good and holy. We want to do what we want, but we're drawn to do what you know is good. There's a tension inside us that we don't like, and Paul helps us see it. We could thank Paul for this tension, this self-awareness. Or we could, like Paul, say "thanks be to God." For inner tension that keeps us true to you. In Christ's name we pray. Amen.

My friend John and I liked to go to the Serbian restaurant on the south side of Chicago when we were in town. It's no longer there, but it will live in our hearts, or our stomachs forever.

Here are some of the features of this memorable place. The center of the restaurant was a circular pit, where the luckiest diners could sit. On special occasions, a Russian singer, with grey beard, fiery eyes, and black satin costume with knee high old leather boots, would come out, plop a bottle of Vodka on the piano, and sing Russian torch songs. There were also real torches on the walls. The owner and the pretty waitresses looked like they had just come out of a vampire movie. In a good way.

Their vegetable soup would have made a vampire into a vegetarian. Everything else was good, too. Yours truly got carried away one night when the music was loud, and spirits were high. I told the owner of the restaurant to bring me a blood transfusion; I wanted to be Serbian. Really. He had me say it again into a microphone, and the crowd roared with approval. Maybe they *were* vampires.

Anyway, the hallmark of any visit to this eatery was what you saw when you arrived there early. Like clockwork, at about 5:45 PM, a middle-aged woman would make her entrance, pausing at the captain's station for effect. Once, she was dressed head to toe in white, large baby blue dots all over her dress. Her hair seemed dyed to match. She stood there for a moment in all her glory, then said, apropos of nothing, "I'm early." For some reason, this struck my friend John and I as outrageously funny, and we got a painful case of the giggles. Served us right.

We went to the Serbian restaurant many times over the years. We always tried to arrive before the lady in her unusual outfits (once she dressed completely in leopard print, including her accessories). She always seemed to enter at 5:45 or so, and she always began her evening by saying, "I'm early." Every single time.

Is this the sort of thing God sees when he looks at us? Just a general, affable, weirdness? Does God get a case of the giggles when we do the things we do? How does God feel about the vampire waitresses, or the Russian singer and his torch songs? Is it all just pretty amusing? Or, is there a problem?

I think there is. And I think that St. Paul, when it comes to the problem of being human, nails it.

Our problem is that we do the things we don't want to do, and don't do the things we want to do. Paul's language has been the object of countless parodies, ("*do be do be do*"), and that's OK. But the problem is still there. And the problem is that we can't align ourselves with a loving God on our own.

St. Paul gives this his best with ancient letter-writing techniques. He uses words like "members," "sin," "law," and "death" and, just so we won't get too comfortable, he keeps us guessing about who he's talking about.

Alright, then. Which one of these words from St. Paul's letter to the Romans should we examine first? How about the word "members?" That will work.

The fact is, St. Paul uses the "I" word to talk about human troubles with sin. He says that his members don't follow along too well or willingly when his brain says, "follow God." He could mean that the different parts of his body have a will of their own, or he could be talking about the Christian community he's in, and how different people can't get with the program when it comes to God's good and gracious will.

That is too complicated for me. I am still trying to figure out why the "I'm Early" lady is perpetually early, and how I can become Serbian. So, I'm going to say that Paul is describing an inner conflict that comes from knowing God, but not being able to follow his loving will. By the way, if you can accept that idea, you've got at least half of Lutheranism. So, I'll say it again. *Paul is describing a personal inner conflict that comes from knowing God but not being able to follow his loving will.*

So, wait a minute! Didn't Jesus die to free us from sin? Isn't that struggle over? Aren't we God's loving children now, with no worries or conflicts? You might have some trouble with that idea in the real world. I know I do.

One of my favorite ways to talk about this conflict comes from when I visited a little old lady for communion. Part of the drama of each visit was when her cat would climb up behind me while I was administering the holy meal and try to bite me on the ear. At least, I thought it was drama. It was my ear. But there was more. The little old lady would spend the first half hour of our visit gossiping! She would trot out the names of all the people she didn't like, and talk about the bad things they were doing, and all their various faults. Then, when she ran out of breath, she would say—every time—"Pastor, I don't know why I need communion. All I do is sit here in my little apartment minding my own business. I don't sin."

After hearing otherwise for 30 minutes, I would advise this: "Go ahead and take communion-just in case." We would both commune. I realized that I was no better nor worse than she was. We both had the St. Paul conflict of body and soul: Parts of me do things that work against God, even though parts of me know and love God's gracious will.

If you share that particular self-awareness, then you might find yourself receiving God's forgiveness with me. What should you bring with you? Horrible remorse for sin? If you want, bring it with you. Or, you could just bring inner conflicts and shortcomings to God, confessing the conflict within you that wants to respond well to God's love. Then, like Paul, you could simply say, "Thanks be to God" and let him take care of it.

Is that possible? I think it is and it is necessary, because the world we have, and the self we have, are more than just a silly, "I'm Early" Lady world of sentiment and thrills. A lot is at stake here.

Can sins really be forgiven? When we are hurt to the core, can we experience peace deep inside, or do we strike out at others, or fold arms defensively, keeping new experiences out?

Can relationships really survive? Once, when I was young, I called my parents after I had hurt a friend. My mother answered.

She listened, and then she told me that once she had done something very bad, but she was forgiven. That's all she said. I wanted to know what she did, so I could focus on others, instead of the maturing world of self-accountability and Christian growth. But, that was all my mother said. She limited her comments so that I would focus on myself with new information; that all people fall short of the glory of God but are redeemed by the cross and resurrection.

It's like the cross is a mirror, too. God holds up this cross-shaped mirror to us. In it, we see our own hurts, and what our sinful selves have done to others. But, from behind this terrible mirror of human life, a small voice speaks. It sounds like it is dying, this little voice. There's not much time left for it to speak. But it does, and the voice says, "Father forgive them. They know not what they do."

St. Paul writes a letter about this to his church in Rome, where there were arguments, and temptations and where there were human beings. He describes our human struggle with sin, our struggle to be like a loving God when we just can't, and then he lifts it up to God with hopeful words, "Thanks be to God."

Maybe he knows that God will take care of the mighty struggle that he introduces into our lives when he comes and loves us, but we can't love that well in return. Maybe he knows all about that. I bet he does. Maybe he also knows how simple I want it to be. Like in that restaurant, where I saw the fun and said, "give me a blood transfusion, I want to be Serbian!" I want to be like you. I want to be transformed without struggle. Not possible.

Instead, God comes with us in our struggles to be loving, or forgiving of others, or forgiving of ourselves. God gives you everything he's got for that struggle to mature and grow. He gives you his son, his cross, that mirror, and that small, dying voice. When you hear that voice, be mindful of what and who you are, like Paul was and don't forget the words that will keep you going. They are Paul's words. They are our own. "Thanks be to God."

28

ALL ABOUT WALKING ON WATER

Matthew 14:22-29

> *Immediately he made the disciples get into the boat and go on*
> *ahead to the other side, while he dismissed the crowds. And*
> *after he had dismissed the crowds, he went up the mountain*
> *by himself to pray. When evening came, he was there alone,*
> *but by this time the boat, battered by the waves, was far*
> *from the land, for the wind was against them. And early in*
> *the morning he came walking toward them on the sea. But*
> *when the disciples saw him walking on the sea, they were*
> *terrified, saying, "It is a ghost!" And they cried out in fear.*
> *But immediately Jesus spoke to them and said, "Take heart, it*
> *is I; do not be afraid." Peter answered him, "Lord, if it is you,*
> *command me to come to you on the water." He said, "Come."*

Jesus, it looks like eleven out of twelve disciples stayed in the boat, and
just one, Peter, walked on water. Doing this, walking on water in the
storm, like you do Jesus, is called leading. You bid us, now and then, to
step out of the boat. To step out in faith. Easy to talk about, but hard to
do. Staying in the boat, hand to the oar, is necessary sometimes, too. In

that case, please call us out of the boat onto the water when you need us. That way, it will be easier to follow you. In Christ's name, Amen.

Ballerinas! Does every little girl want to be a ballerina? My daughter did. Her friends all did, too. You know what is required, perhaps: the parental involvement, the costume for rehearsals, the costumes for the recital. Rehearsal and recital fees. The dance shoes, with or without blocks of wood in the toes for going on point. More was involved: driving your ballerina to rehearsals and to the little shop in an out-of-the-way strip mall to buy the very expensive shoes and tights and leotards all in pink. All part of making your little girl's dream of being a beautiful princess come alive. Then, the crush of parents at the recital, all wanting a picture of their little ballerinas. How did we ever survive?

My daughter took dance lessons for years. I got to know the other parents at the little rehearsal hall, with the wall of floor-to-ceiling mirrors and the ballet barre. Rehearsals consisted of teaching cute little girls to dance across the stage, from back to front, and to do a little leap in the center, for which I have forgotten the French name. A jete', I believe, and that's not the important part, either. At my daughter's recital, the other little girls lost their nerve. They would dance half way across the stage in the old theatre downtown, then they would notice the audience and lose their nerve. Instead of making their leap, or jete', or whatever it is, into the air, then continuing to cross, they would stop dead, then just wander away.

My daughter took charge in the midst of a growing ballerina panic. While the other little girls froze with stage fright, my daughter started to the center, where I saw her look back at the other little girls. Her look seemed to say, "Get a hold of yourselves, ballerinas! This is about more than pink tights and showing off. We've got a show to do!"

Then, a split second later, she executed her leap, landed properly, and danced away to the other corner of the stage.

I learned something about my daughter that day. I saw something new in her, something that has never failed her, through marriage, motherhood, jobs, divorce, and later, planning her dream wedding. She stays with the program. She doesn't get flustered.

Speaking in gospel terms, from the episode in boat and on water with Jesus and Peter, it's like this: *step out in faith when Jesus calls.*

Now, the disciples, and anyone else rowing that boat through the storm at sea, might not like being compared to a bunch of little girls in ballerina outfits, on the stage of life. But, something has to happen, and that's the first step.

Here's the story, straight from the gospel of Matthew. Jesus has fed the 5,000. Please remember, the point of the story and what made it work was Jesus asking for the disciples to help with the food. We could also say that Jesus asked them to *participate in their own faith*. Not to panic. Not to go all negative about the problems around them, but to do something that Jesus could bless and share. He taught them well. It worked out that everyone was fed, and, by all accounts, we saw the invention of leftovers (twelve baskets full.) All in all, it was a good day. A good day for everyone.

Next thing you know, Jesus goes and does something else unexpected. It's actually hard to explain. Jesus goes up some mountain and prays to his Heavenly Father. Before he goes, he sends these same disciples out in a boat. Wait, though. I forgot something. Jesus sends disciples in a boat out on the Sea of Galilee alone. Without him.

Not being one of the major seas, or even a second-rate ocean, you might think the Sea of Galilee was and is relatively harmless. Not so! The wind and the waves could whip up the Galilean Sea without even a moment's notice, so that a once calm body of water could become treacherous, a killing force for experienced sea-goers. You could die out there.

Why did Jesus send his disciples out there alone, without *him*? It doesn't seem like a good idea, Jesus! This isn't the old TV show Gilligan's Island, where a three-hour tour turns into a storm at sea and it turns out that the professor can make anything out of coconuts and Mrs. Howell really does have enough clothes to get by. This is real life. And, Jesus, you are saying that real life is about you standing away from us, on the horizon, and someone walking on the water, the way you do, to cope with the storm. Yes, that is what you are saying, Jesus. And may I add, I don't see it that way. Not for me. Look for me in the boat, doing a little practical cowering and some rowing. Don't look for me on the water, walking, leading … yes, that's it. Leading. I'm telling you that you made a person like Peter a leader that day, and I want no part of it!

Jesus, we need to talk.

I guess the first time I thought about leadership at all for ordinary people, it was my father I thought about. He was late for dinner that night, and I asked my mother why. It turned out that my dad had heard about an emergency. A boy—someone like me—decided to walk through an old, abandoned house. The floor gave way, and the boy fell through. He cut his arm badly and lost a lot of blood before they heard his cries and found him.

The call went out across the community for donors to give blood. No one in our family had ever done anything like this before. But my father did. It was like he heard a call, and stepped out his ordinary life, and followed.

My boyhood imagination ran wild waiting for my father to come home that night. I imagined the needle sticking his arm, the blood flowing out, hurting him, going into the little boy. It was more complicated than that, of course, and simpler, too. Years later I brought it up again, and my father told me it was nothing. I shared with him how impressed I was as a child with his trying something new, his sacrifice. I told him it shaped a part of me and my life.

He was uncomfortable with this attention and changed the subject. But now, today, let's keep the subject alive and the conversation going. What does it mean to hear Christ calling, saying, "Take heart. It is I. Do not be afraid. Come!"

What *does* it mean? Can this be a message for everybody? Isn't this sort of thing just for people who might be the next church council president, or run the altar guild, or maybe get called into the ordained ministry? In that case, it would not be for any of us, you might think.

Matthew, the gospel writer, probably knew a lot of people who thought just like that. After all, he was writing to a church full of people who used to be Jews, but who were now Christians. They probably didn't know what to make of that, let alone think about if God was calling them to something out of the ordinary in life. Matthew remembered times in Peter's life when Jesus backed off just enough so that his most unpredictable disciple could follow him. Across a stormy sea. Or, through the storms of an everyday, average church. Or, an ordinary, everyday life.

For now, here is something I want you to know. If I believed that leading in the church was just for council presidents and ordained pastors and certain others, I wouldn't be an ordained minister at all. I would have trained for a profession where I could make things happen all by myself. But that isn't Jesus' way with us. He keeps calling to us, drawing us out of what we were and where we were comfortable. Jesus keeps calling to us and asking us to step out of the boat and into the storm. Jesus is waiting. It's a foregone conclusion that anyone who tries to be a leader in this kind of world is going to sink sometimes and look like a fool or feel like one from time to time. The Bible says that Jesus picks us up when we get that sinking feeling and keeps us going.

Speaking of stepping out of the boat and that sinking feeling that goes with it, I haven't told you what happened the day after my daughter's recital. All the parents went to the dance studio to pick up their kids' things. It was locked and dark, when we were expecting the instructor to be there. Word quickly spread that she had taken the box office receipts from the recital and run away with the guy who did the lighting.

There was talk among the parents about "what next?" Someone suggested that we work together, find a new instructor, and run the studio ourselves. There was a decisive moment when just one person could have stepped forward to lead the way. Maybe God was calling such a person, right then, if you believe in how Jesus worked with say, Peter in the boat. But no one stepped forward, and sadly, all the little girls went home. That was that.

Jesus wants to ensure that this does not happen with his church. So, he starts out with a boat, and a storm, and a guy named Peter who probably couldn't even swim. And Jesus called him to come out on the water, to walk, to step out in faith, and to lead. He has never stopped calling people in this way, even you, even me.

29

FAITH OR *FAITH*

Matthew 15:28

Then Jesus answered her, "Woman, great is your faith! Let it be done for you as you wish." And her daughter was healed instantly.

Jesus, everyone tells me that I ought to have more faith. I tell myself this as well. If I had more, then things would go well with me, and I would understand when they did not go well. Or, is faith when Jesus and I lock horns, like the woman and Jesus in the gospel story? Or, is faith sitting quietly, obediently taking what comes? No, I think that the last one is the least faith. Jesus likes it when I speak up to him. Amen.

I was a chaplain in training once, and after the training was complete, I decided to go back into parish ministry. The reasons for that aren't important now, but what happened in the training is important.

One morning, before our work began, all of the chaplains were sitting around and having coffee. We were talking, and in came the head chaplain. He was a very authoritative figure, full of insight, and he tended to galvanize the group. That is exactly what happened on that particular morning.

Another chaplain started the day in an angry mood. He wanted to be hired in a paid position at that hospital after the training was over. So, he spoke up to the head chaplain. He said, "I need special consideration here. I've given up time at my other job, I've stayed late, come in on my day off, and gone the extra mile. I need special consideration for a chaplain job here."

Now, here comes the most interesting part. The man continued: "God knows how much I've done for him. He knows how much I've given him. I'm going to ask God for a job here, and I have the right to do that. God needs to give me this job. We have a relationship here. I can ask him for something and expect to get it."

My mouth was hanging open. I was astonished. I was shocked, yes shocked. You don't demand things from God. God is not a busboy, who will bring you another glass of water, or even a waiter. The faith that I was taught says that you wait nicely, uncomplainingly for whatever God will give you, and then you ask God to help you make the best of it.

So, which is it? Are you chaplain A, who knows that he's served God and asks for something out of that longstanding relationship? Is that alright? Is it proper?

Or, are you like Chaplain B (me), who serves God just as faithfully, but never dares to ask God for anything, just to persevere for whatever God sends? Which is it, A or B? I'd like to know.

Maybe God can straighten this out via the gospel. The story today comes in two parts, each related to one another, each equally complicated (which means that if I read them fast like I usually do, they don't make sense).

Slower readings produce some details.

Like I said, the gospel story for today comes in two parts. The first part has the party of the first part be the disciples. It looks like they have religion and faith confused, just like many of us do. In religion, your worth comes from what you take in. Pure foods, pure thoughts, pure doctrine.

Old religion, in the Lutheran church anyway, was all about having the correct facts about God. Please let me go on record as having dedicated my life to having the best information possible about God, sin, grace, and salvation. It's important. But it's not the whole picture.

Some in our church seem to have a fascination with the branch of our denomination—the people from Missouri—who keep people away from communion (and even, perhaps, heaven) because the beliefs that go into their heads are not correct enough yet , in alignment with those from the Missouri branch. We exclaim, "How can they do this? What's the matter with them?" Doubtless, we could read through the first half of the gospel for today, where disciples seem to be worried about "the things that go into a person keeping them pure." We would draw certain parallels between their lack of understanding and the prohibitive, restrictive Lutherans we know now. How, we wonder, can they be so, well, so restrictive, so prohibitive?

But what's the alternative? Jesus says that it isn't the pure food, or the pure doctrine that we pour into ourselves that makes us good. He says it's what comes out of our mouths, and out of our hearts that matters. As a master of Lutheran theology, and of the spontaneous wisecrack, I think this means that I am in deep trouble. In order to be good, I should always sound like the inscriptions at the base of Precious Moments figures. Extra sugary sweet. It's not going to happen. So, what then?

What, then, is faith?

Remember Chaplain A. The one who was good at demanding things from God? Well, meet his sister (his sister in the faith, anyway), the woman from Canaan. She's the one in the second half of the gospel.

She's the one who has a child in terrible trouble, the kind that only God can help. The child is possessed by a demon.

So, she asks Jesus for help. No, that's not what she does. I know how I'd do that. I would be the nice Chaplain B, who tags along behind my savior and asks for whatever it takes to deal with my "demon child" problem. That would be me. This woman is different.

She pesters Jesus. She won't let him alone. She is his major headache for the day. The disciples say, "Send her away, for she keeps shouting after us."

Finally, it comes down to this. The woman confronts Jesus. She gets in his face. We would say that she is "proactive," and that is important. In other words, she is prepared to do whatever it takes to get a cure for her daughter. That is different, worlds away, from a passive stance before God that says, "Oh, whatever." The woman here wants this problem solved.

Jesus finally gives her his attention. She speaks to him on her knees, which looks like humility, means worship, and keeps the conversation rolling. Is this faith? Let's see.

Jesus says that she's like a dog at the table of the chosen people. Yes—that's exactly what he says. It is not a compliment. And, no one understands what it means. Is Jesus really limiting his ministry to just his own people only? Only insiders get to reach Jesus?

It couldn't be … but it sounds like it! Maybe that's it.

The woman couldn't care less. She's got a problem! Jesus needs to solve it. She says that she'll gladly take the dogfood-like crumbs from God's table. And her daughter is healed.

Which brings us back to now.

Help me decide. Is faith in Jesus more like Chaplain A, who demands that God give him what he needs? Or, is faith in Jesus more like Chaplain B, who (and I have this on good authority, since Chaplain B is me) would rather bear life's burdens obediently and ask Jesus for nothing more than the strength to bear difficult burdens?

Is faith being polite to Jesus, or giving him a headache with our requests, demands, and entreaties?

It seems, in the final analysis, that crumbs from God' table are enough to answer prayer, and make life better, if you have the guts to keep asking, even demanding. Jesus says that it's what comes out of our mouths that count. Will your faith sound more like Chaplain A, or Chaplain B?

AFTERWORD

The great Dorothy Parker used to review books for a living. Perhaps after reading this one, you'd agree with something Parker wrote about some other book, whose title doesn't come to mind. But the quote does: "This is not a novel to be tossed aside lightly. It should be thrown with great force." So it may be here.

When most of the essays in this book first appeared, they were sermons. At the time, a lot of the people who heard them found out that they were uncomfortable, to say the least, with ambiguity and a wry sense of humor when it came to God. I think that these things are necessary means to approach our side of that relationship. Maybe you feel the same. If true, then many thanks go to my wife, Melissa, for encouraging me over many years of learning how to write this way and believing that other people would like to approach God this way.

Some years ago, I was asked to deliver a keynote address at a big national assembly. I'd never done such a thing before, so I labored to assemble about forty minutes of material that sounded religious enough. Yet, when I was delivering my speech, I had the nagging feeling that something was missing. So, I departed from my text and sang this song, to the astonishment of those who were still listening. The lyrics are by a man named Lorenz Hart, who also had an unusual way of looking at life. I'll leave it to you to say if it has anything to do with our ongoing, trial and error, yet graceful walk with God.

If they asked me, I could write a book
About the way you walk and whisper and look
I could write a preface on how we met
So, the world would never forget

And the simple secret of the plot
Is just to tell them that I love you a lot
And the world discovers, as my book ends
How to make two lovers of friends

Richard W. Dow
Orange Park, FL

Postscript

Now that your ride in the *Red Convertible* has come to an end, let me take a moment to tell you why this book came to print.

I will have been married to the author for 42 years by the time this book is published, and I have been with him in all of the churches he has served. In each instance, the people have not only listened politely to the Pastor, as good Lutherans are taught to do; many remember what he said, took notes, and quoted him days later!

Some would comment to me how much they love his stories and that his style of preaching can help them connect the teachings of Jesus to their real life. Many have asked for copies of the sermons. What a blessing!

What you may not know is that Pastor Dow doesn't think anyone really wants to read "a bunch of old sermons." I know better and, loving wife that I am, I encouraged him to write this book, and I'd love *Red Convertible* to prove him wrong.

Let us know your thoughts. Email us at RedConvertible2018@gmail.com or share your reviews on Amazon.com.

I hope that this book has blessed your life. Now, go, carry the message, carry the Light!

Soli Deo Gloria, Glory to God alone.

Melissa Dow

Richard Dow is an ordained Lutheran pastor currently serving as a consultant in interim ministry for the Florida-Bahama Synod of the Evangelical Lutheran Church in America (ELCA). He has taught public speaking and religions at a local college and has a love of classic cars and old movies.

As a gifted storyteller with a plethora of stories gathered from life experience and nearly forty years in parish ministry, Pastor Dow effortlessly weaves the Gospel throughout his writing. You will almost hear him speaking as you read this book.

Made in the USA
Columbia, SC
09 November 2018